How to Sound Like A Million Dollars

Lyle V. Mayer
How to Sound Like A Million Dollars

Turning
Your Everyday Voice
Into
an Asset

WALKER AND COMPANY
New York

Copyright © 1986 by Lyle V. Mayer

All rights reserved. No part of this book may be reproduced or transmitted in any form or by any means, electronic or mechanical, including photocopying, recording, or by any information storage and retrieval system, without permission in writing from the Publisher.

First published in the United States of America in 1986 by the Walker Publishing Company, Inc.

Published simultaneously in Canada by John Wiley & Sons Canada, Limited, Rexdale, Ontario.

Library of Congress Cataloging-in-Publication Data

Mayer, Lyle Vernon, 1916-
  How to sound like a million dollars.

  Includes index.
  1. Voice culture—Exercises. I. Title.
PN4197.M384 1986   808.5   86-13146
ISBN 0-8027-0922-2
ISBN 0-8027-7295-1 (paperback)

Printed in the United States of America
10 9 8 7 6 5 4 3 2 1

Book design by Lorraine Mullaney

Contents

INTRODUCTION:
How to take control of your voice   1
How to use this book

1
Why Read This Book?   5

Evaluating your voice • What improvement you'll see when you're finished • How you say it makes more of an impression than what you say • Irritating voices turn people off • You *can* improve your voice • What kind of speaking voice turns people on? • Hearing how you come across to others • Unpleasant vocal qualities • Articulation • Volume • Vocal pizazz • Foreign and regional accents • Evaluate someone else's voice • Record your voice • Evaluating the recording

2
Sound Off!   25

Correct breathing • Stress and tension in your voice • Loosening up

3

Put Your Best Voice Forward! 36

Is your voice pleasant to listen to? • Free up the sound • Using your lips correctly • How to focus the tone • Overcoming the seven most common voice flaws: breathiness, stridency, harshness, nasality, denasality, throatiness, hoarseness

4

Conserve Your Consonants 66

The importance of consonants in good speech • Your head's "parts of speech": lips, front teeth, lower jaw, tongue • Using these effectively • Voiced and voiceless consonants • The eighteen troublemaking consonants • The plosives: t,d,p,b,k,g • The glides: w,l,r • The nasals: m,n,ng • The fricatives: s,z,th,th,f,y

5

Varnish Your Vowels 124

The vowels • The four unruly vowel sounds: a as in ask, ee as in feet, i as in fit, e as in bet

6

Discipline Your Diphthongs 139

i as in ice • ow as in down • oi as in point

7

Speak Up! 147

Speech that's too low in volume • Projection • Slow

down on the words ● Pitch level ● Avoiding unpleasant speech patterns ● Don't strain your throat ● Don'ts and dos ● Using variation in volume effectively

8
Be Vibrant, Varied, Vivid, and Versatile!   161

The drone's gallery ● Give your voice some get-up-and-go! ● Slide and glide ● Hop, skip, and jump! ● Gadgets and gewgaws ● Upsie-Downsie? Get off the seesaw! ● Don't dash! Don't dawdle! Regulate your rate! ● The pause that refreshes ● Getting your act together

Post Mortem   196

Make an After record ● Compare your recordings ● Evaluate the new record ● Note your improvement

Index   199

How to Sound Like A Million Dollars

Introduction: How to Take Control of Your Voice

People who have poor speaking voices—the kind that set your teeth on edge—are almost always unaware of this. We are our most enchanted listeners, and it's human nature for each of us to believe that nobody speaks as well as we do.

Try to hear what voice problems you have! Be hard on yourself!

How do you go about this?

You gaze into a mirror six or seven times a day. You check your hair, your necktie, or your makeup. But how often do you check your speech in a voice mirror? I'm talking about a tape recorder, of course. And a tape recorder is essential and indispensable as far as you're concerned. Beg, borrow, or buy one. The market is flooded with small, inexpensive recorders, and a good one is worth its weight in gold. You can tape yourself dozens of times and monitor your progress as you go through this book. A mirror doesn't lie. Neither does a tape recorder.

Important! Impose on a patient, indefatigable friend, spouse, relative, or roommate. Ask this person to help you judge and pass sentence on your voice. A tape recorder has one drawback. For example: If loudness—particularly the lack of—is one of your problems, you may automatically turn up the volume when you record or play back. A whisper can easily be converted to a roar. Thus, the recorded sound you hear always seems as loud as World War II to your own ears. That's why another judge comes in handy.

d of caution: make sure that your friendly critic isn't too friendly. Select somebody who is honest and brutally candid—who'll tell you what you *need* to hear and not what you *want* to hear. You're asking the person to be a referee or a connoisseur, not a sympathetic witness.

Want to have some fun? Try the Buddy System. Choose a partner who's interested in improving his or her own speaking voice. (It's even more fun if you have a couple of partners.) Not only can you check each other, but this also gives you a chance to retaliate!

PROGRAM YOURSELF!

Read one chapter at a sitting. Then halt. Go back and try the exercises.

If possible, set up a regular schedule for yourself. I heartily recommend an hour a day for practicing. If you can't afford that much time, even a few minutes a day with your vocal push-ups will be helpful. After you become familiar with some of the exercises, you'll be able to run through them while showering, shaving, or blow-drying your hair.

Allow yourself at least one to two weeks per chapter. More if you think necessary. *Don't move on to another chapter until you show definite improvement.* How will you know when you've improved? More taping. And more critical and candid comments from your collaborator. Be patient. I'm asking you to alter some lifetime habits. This isn't easy. Hang in there! You'll improve!

At the end of Chapter 1, material is provided so that you can tape yourself. Play it back. This will give you an excellent idea of how you sound in general. Use the self-evaluation chart. But be tough on yourself. Ask your partner(s) to be supercritical. *After* you've determined what your problems are, move on.

Have you discovered that you talk through your nose? Do you have a nasal, foghorn, or whiny quality? Is your voice hard, tense, and strident? Do you sound growly, gravelly, or hoarse? Are you breathy and whispery? Read Chapter 3: Put Your Best Voice Forward! Tape one of the selections. If you have no problems, skip to the next chapter. But if you do, find the section that addresses your problem. Tape again. Then get to work on the specific exercises that will help you eliminate the undesirable vocal quality. This may take an hour, five hours, two weeks. Stay with it until you've licked the problem. Your recorder and your friend will tell you when.

Mumble, mangle, or swallow your words? Sound as if your mouth is full of wet tissue paper? One by one, do Chapter 4: Conserve Your Consonants; 5: Varnish Your Vowels; 6: Discipline Your Diphthongs.

Don't be disheartened if you discover that your speech isn't as distinct and intelligible as you thought it was. Join the crowd! More people have problems with articulation than any other area of voice or speech.

Even if you feel that you have flawless diction, run through every exercise in these three chapters. Tape the two stories: "The Haunted House" and "Knock Thrice Before You Enter."

Play back and listen carefully. If certain sounds trouble you, repeat the recommended practice material that will help you correct the problem. Don't hurry through Chapters 4–6. Linger. *You may find it necessary to spend more time with these chapters than you do with the rest of the book.*

Do you talk too softly? Is your voice marshmallowy, wan, and weak? A partner will be even more helpful than a recorder. Select material from Chapter 7: Speak Up! Read it in the largest room you can find. Station your friend at the opposite end of the room and let him judge how well your voice carries. If it carries well, jump to the next chapter. If it doesn't, stay awhile. Building a mousy voice into a strong one takes time. Don't rush the process. A gradual, step-by-step approach is best, and this chapter will show you how.

Are you a Jane-or-Johnny-One-Note? Sound bored with yourself? Speak at a rate that turns words into greased bullets?

Or is your speaking rate draggy and funereal? Even if your answer is **NO,** you'll enjoy reading the exercises in Chapter 8: Be Vibrant, Varied, Vivid, and Versatile! But if your answer is **YES,** a week or two with the practice material will add punch and ginger to your speaking.

I've saved the hardest part for last. The Big Challenge: Your taped sessions will prove that you've made remarkable progress retraining your voice. Can you carry over these improvements into your everyday vocal communication? *And can you make them stick?*

You're about to read eight chapters. As far as your voice personality is concerned, these will be the most important chapters you'll ever read.

Are you ready?

1
Why Read This Book?

Ask yourself the following questions. Check the appropriate answer. Be honest.
 (Make two photocopies—one for your listening friend—and fill out the checklist on them—not on the one in the book.)

WHAT'S THE PAYOFF? WHAT WILL I BE ABLE TO DO AFTER I FINISH THIS BOOK THAT I CAN'T DO PRETTY WELL RIGHT NOW?
You'll be able to talk a great deal better—that's what. You'll improve the quality of your talking. How important is that? Take note: this is not another book about public speaking. It's a book that will give you an advantage every day of your life, not just on those rare occasions when you may have to get up and talk to an audience.
 Do you realize how much just plain talking you do?
 About 30,000 words a day! That's equivalent to half a dozen books a week. In one year more than 11,000,000 words will pour out of your mouth! If you live to be seventy, you'll have devoted thirteen years of your life just to speaking!
 Are you a career person, or are you planning a career? Take your pick: carhop or carpenter, data processor or doctor, nurse or nuclear physicist, cop or coffin-maker, lawyer or librarian, teacher or tambourine player, actor or archbishop. Better plan to do a lot of chattering.

5

HOW TO SOUND LIKE A MILLION DOLLARS

HOW OFTEN DO PEOPLE ASK YOU TO...	FREQUENTLY	NOW AND THEN	NEVER
Repeat what you've just said?			
Speak up because they can't hear you?			
Slow down?			
HOW OFTEN DO PEOPLE TELL YOU THAT YOU...			
Talk too loudly?			
Speak with an accent or dialect?			
Sound tense or nervous?			
Mumble?			
HOW OFTEN DO PEOPLE...			
Misunderstand you?			
HOW OFTEN DO YOU...			
Stumble?			
Come away from a conversation wishing you had been more convincing?			
Feel that you've made a bad impression?			
Find your listener's attention wandering while you're speaking?			

Each FREQUENTLY you checked counts 2.
Each NOW AND THEN you checked counts 1.
Each NEVER you checked counts 0.

If your score falls between—
   1 and 8: Read the book for fun and enjoyment. Here and there you'll want to touch up or add a little polish to your voice.
   9 and 16: Read it and then get to work on the particular exercises that are recommended specifically for you.
   17 and 24: Read and re-read! Half—maybe more—of the exercises will tune you up.

The way in which you express yourself tells the world a lot about you. Successful communication depends mostly on the effective use of voice. And consider this: Your daily conversation isn't devoted entirely to subjects of earthshaking significance. A lot of it, frankly, is about unexciting, trivial, and piddling subjects. That's why it's so important to know how to give your voice some zip and zing! An effervescent, buoyant voice can make the most humdrum and rinky-dink subjects seem lively and invigorating.

Beauty Isn't in the Eye of the Onlooker. It's in the Ear of the Listener!

A prominent Beverly Hills, California speech communication specialist conducted a fascinating study. The results convinced Dr. Lillian Glass that the way we talk is of far greater importance than the way we look.

Dr. Glass selected two groups of people of ten each. Each group was to be judged, although the individuals were not told how and why they were being appraised.

The first group consisted of attractive people. But they

all had poor speaking voices—abrasive or fuzzy—and anemic articulation. A volunteer jury sized up this group as *unattractive*.

The second group were average-looking, but each of them had a melodious voice and clean-as-a-whistle articulation. How did the jury rate them? *Attractive!*

A few years back my wife worked for an employment agency in San Francisco, calling as many as 150 corporations or small businesses each day to seek job listings. She soon discovered that one-third of the receptionists, who provide the first business contact with a company, had unpleasant speaking voices or were totally unintelligible. They battered the names of the very companies who paid their salaries. Marilyn Person Smith, she learned, was Merrill Lynch Pierce Fenner and Smith. The Oh Noy Lassner Vision was, in reality, the Owens-Illinois Glass Container Division.

And can you figure this one out? Gunnery War Ickle Armen? Translation: Montgomery Ward Optical Department.

These same sloppy Joes and Josephines pepper their business dialogue with such gems as: "Whoja wanna talk ta?" "Gimme yer name agin," and "He's on uner line. Woncha hang on a mint?" "Whajasay?"

It makes no difference if one is executive vice president, personnel director, or custodian. Bungled speech or a creaky, grubby voice, face-to-face or via the telephone, turns off potential customers.

A General Motors vice president stated in a letter to me:

> I hire, fire, and promote people, and I find it quite appalling that the reason I don't hire many of them in the first place is not so much *what* they say during the interview as *how* they say it. I have no time for mumblers—those with a mouthful of mush and a dumpling in the throat. And then there are the Minnie or Mickey Mouse voices—so watery and thin that, even though I sit about four feet from them, I can't hear half of what they say (and my doctor tells me I have 20-20 hearing!). Maybe worst of all is the hopeful interviewee with the raw and scratchy voice. It's like running your fingernails up and down a chalkboard.

WHY READ THIS BOOK?

How you say what you say rather than *what* you say forms a lasting and almost permanent impression. Your voice is the sharp cutting edge of your personality.

First impressions, not to mention second and third, do count! And have you noticed? Once you form an impression of a person—even though you may be wrong—it's difficult to change your opinion.

People Tune Out Irritating Voices!

We persist in thinking, for example, that an ear-piercing voice signifies a disagreeable personality. A shrill, strident, metallic vocal quality is supposed to belong to a person who is uptight, taut, or neurotic—an individual to be avoided. This isn't always true.

A pale, weak, or too-soft speaking voice suggests that its owner has a cotton-candy personality, completely lacking in character and guts, even though that may be far from the case. Jacqueline Onassis has a feathery, whispery voice (although no one would accuse her of being gutless).

Nevertheless, your listeners often jump to hasty conclusions about your personality on the basis of listening to you talk for only a few minutes. Pleasing speech habits increase your chances of social and professional success and open the door to a more fulfilling life.

Dorothy Sarnoff, Broadway and opera star, and speech consultant, puts it in a nutshell: "If you're single, your speech may decide whether you'll ever marry. If you're married, your speech may decide whether you stay that way."

Yes, but—*I've been talking for quite a few years—almost since the day I was born. If there's something wrong with the way I talk, why haven't I been told about it before now?*

Your friends, spouse, and siblings hear you all the time. They get used to the way you speak. You may have clogged speech, a galling, whiny, one-half decibel voice. But your peers and relatives probably like you in spite of all these faults. And they wouldn't be your friends if they continually harped at you about your shortcomings.

Yes, but—*Even if my voice isn't as good as it should be, it works! I've been communicating with people all of my life.*

The voice you've grown up with and that you use now may be depriving you of the real advantages you'd get from the voice nature intended you to have!

Robert Burns, in his wise little poem "To a Louse," says:

> Oh, would some power the gift give us,
> To see ourselves as others see us!

Have you ever seen yourself in home movies or on TV? Startled? Embarrassed? You didn't realize, did you, that you walked with a list, used choppy little gestures, slouched, and waggled your eyebrows while talking.

Let's alter two words in Burns's poem: "Oh, would some power the gift give us, to *hear* ourselves as others *hear* us!"

The first time you listen to a recording of your voice may be an even greater shock than seeing yourself on a screen. You'll probably say, "That couldn't be me!" "Do I talk that fast?" "I didn't realize my voice was that high." "I don't sound like that!"

Indeed, you don't sound like that *to yourself*. But alas, there's the evidence. You do sound like that!

CAN I ACTUALLY CHANGE MY VOICE?

Yes!

Perhaps *improve* is a better word. Nothing physical will change. Your Adam's apple won't get bigger or suddenly disappear. But in this book you'll discover ways and means of taking the basic equipment you already have and using it with maximum efficiency. Golfers can better their strokes, sopranos can learn to hit high notes without screeching, and sprinters can shorten their running times. When you've finished the book and practiced the recommended exercises, you'll have acquired the charisma of a new voice, one that is more likable and appealing than your present speaking voice.

How do I go about improving?
The largest room in the world is the room for improvement!

This book is loaded with down-to-earth, practical, nontechnical drills and exercises. The exercises are not dull vocal gymnastics. Most of them are humorous. You'll find them enjoyable to read and fun to do. They're also helpful. They work!

I've tested every exercise in this book for about a third of a century. They've been successful with more than 5,000 human beings, from older adults—major generals and grandmothers among them—to yuppies, groupies, and college-age crowds. An overwhelming majority of these individuals made remarkable improvement in their speaking voices, an improvement clearly demonstrated by their "before and after" recordings.

Follow the simple instructions carefully and then practice, *practice*, PRACTICE!

The eye-popping performances of the Miami Dolphins, the Edmonton Oilers, or the Los Angeles Lakers are not spur-of-the-moment inspirations. They are the result of endless, grueling hours of practice long before the season starts.

Carl Lewis, 1984 Olympic gold medal winner, was asked how many years he'd spent developing his tremendous athletic skills. He replied, "The day I stopped crawling I took up running."

Meryl Streep wasn't born a fine actress or John McEnroe a gifted (if quirky) tennis player. Linda Ronstadt didn't come into the world a delightful song stylist. Soprano Leona Mitchell rehearses an operatic role for two years before she sings it at the Met.

These people plodded and struggled for years before they

hit the jackpot. As the wheezy old saying goes: "Genius is ninety-nine percent perspiration and one percent inspiration."

Few of us are born with great speaking voices. Certainly there are individuals who have the gift. Even these people, however, can improve their natural gifts with a little extra effort.

Nobody ever does his best. That's why we all have an excellent chance to do better.

WHAT KIND OF A SPEAKING VOICE TURNS PEOPLE ON?

The ten best speaking voices in America according to a recent survey of 500 speech communication experts: Sean Connery, Julie Andrews, John Gielgud, Connie Chung, James Earl Jones, Joan Collins, Gregory Peck, Pernell Roberts, Paul Harvey, and John Chancellor.

Here are voices that enthrall and hypnotize us—voices that command attention.

A Top-Notch Speaking Voice Has a Pleasing Quality

Quality is the tone color or texture of a voice.

Kathleen Battle, rising young opera star, and Barbra Streisand and Olivia Newton-John, of less Olympian heights, have at least one thing in common. Each of them is a soprano. Yet, if each made a recording of "America the Beautiful" and sang it in the same key, few of us would confuse one singer with either of the others.

Likewise, if a trumpet player, a violinist, and a saxophonist played middle C and held the tone for the same length of time and at the same loudness level, you'd have no problem recognizing which was which.

And if a close friend phones you, you can generally identify the person at once. Perhaps there's a warmth and richness about that particular voice. Another friend's voice, however, is hard and steely. Still another's voice is hoarse and raspy, and a fourth friend who calls has a muted and misty voice. All of these terms help us identify quality.

You already know much about yourself, but primarily from the inside out. Maybe it's a bit of a shock to be told that you come across to others as arrogant, aloof, sarcastic, or bitchy when you really don't have the slightest desire to create that kind of impression.

"There is no index of character so sure as the human voice," British Prime Minister Benjamin Disraeli once remarked.

Here's a hit list of shabby, obnoxious vocal qualities. Although vocal peculiarities are exploited by some celebrities, for the rest of us these quality quirks are undesirable in everyday life.

BREATHY Feathery, frizzy, and fluffy. Breath seems to be leaking out. What exits from the mouth is not so much solid words as cotton puffballs. The late Marilyn Monroe had a downy, wafer-thin little voice.

STRIDENT Brassy, tense, edgy, and sometimes rather high-pitched. The voice seems tight, as if it were produced by a pressure cooker. Joan Rivers, to some, is strident.

HARSH Rough, rasping, gravelly, and often rather low-pitched, reminding you of rusty hinges and creaky doors in slasher movies. This voice suggests that its owner is angry. George C. Scott used this growly quality to great effect in his Oscar-winning movie about the World War II general George S. Patton.

NASAL Talking through the nose—a nasal twang. The voice has a foghorn, sometimes a wailing, quality. Many singers of country music adore it. Try the Nashville Network, the Oak Ridge Boys, Porter Waggoner, and Willie Nelson.

Throaty   Hollow, muffled, thick—generally a low-pitched rumble. It's the voice from the rear of the vacuum cleaner. Walt Disney's Goofy and other cartoon characters often use it. (Which way did he go, George? Which way did he go?)

Hoarse   Noisy, scratchy, raw, strained. The owner of a hoarse voice doesn't talk—he croaks. Hoarseness hints that the person either has a bad case of laryngitis or needs to clear his throat. Those two feisty old gentlemen in "The Muppets," Statler and Waldorf, are colorful examples.

Now, as far as we've gone, do you feel that you might be a candidate for the hit list? Don't despair! Each of these defects of *QUALITY* will be tackled individually in Chapter 3. You'll be given lots of help. Read on.

A First-Rate Speaking Voice Is Distinct, Intelligible, and Easy to Understand.

Articulation must be as sharp and incisive as a laser beam. (Articulation, enunciation, and diction, for all practical purposes, mean the same thing.)

Feeble articulation is our numero uno problem as far as voice and speech are concerned. *Lazy lips!* The word *mumbling* is often used to describe careless, sluggish articulation. The more you gobble your words, the more indistinct you become. Mumblers don't open their mouths. Their lips, which have as much spring and bounce as two pieces of stale liver, never move. These word-wreckers drop or omit sounds:

give me is heard as *gimme*
thinking becomes *thinkin'*
going to changes to *gunna'*
understand turns into *unnerstan'*

WHY READ THIS BOOK?

Garblers are first cousins of mumblers. They mangle sounds or add extra, unwanted sounds:

length, strength alter to *lenth, strenth*
across becomes *acrosst*

A popular movie star—his pictures break box office records—loves to play the underdog who battles his way to the top. Mr. Macho deserves a double Oscar. He's the only Hollywood actor who can mumble and garble simultaneously. A TV movie critic remarked about one of the star's recent, sizzling hits:

> The problem with him is not that he can't act. It's that he can't speak. He sounds as if he has a mouth full of Elmer's glue. In his current epic, he emits Tarzanlike grunts and yowls through most of the picture.

This is O.K. with audiences, because they don't expect grunts and yowls to make sense. But at the end of the movie, to give the film social significance, he delivers a message. At this point the movie falls flat on its face, along with anybody in the audience who is trying to figure out what the man is saying.

How do you develop athletic *articulation?* Check out Chapters 4, 5, and 6. For many of you, these may be the most important chapters in the book.

An Outstanding Speaking Voice Is Easily Heard

"What did you say?" Do your friends often ask you that? It's likely that you're not talking loudly enough.

Loudness means volume, projection, intensity.

You might have beautiful enunciation and still be unable to reach your listeners. A voice that is excessively faint or frail annoys most people. It also labels you as timid and weak-kneed.

The head of the economics department of a large eastern university had a problem: A new, young instructor—a Ph.D. and *magna cum laude* Harvard graduate—was doing miserably in the classroom. Student complaints were many and bitter. (Outside the classroom they called him Dr. Dovetonsils.) Would I drop in on one of his classes and observe? I did. Dr. Dovetonsils had a scrawny, mousy little voice. He was underprojecting. Over the next two weeks I spent about four hours with him, teaching him to speak with more vim and vigor. His students were amazed at the difference. He became an admired and successful teacher. Dr. Dovetonsils metamorphosed into Dr. Dauntless.

Too loud is as hard on your listeners as too soft. Have you ever run into a boomer? This one could easily make a speech in the Houston Astrodome without a mike, and nobody would miss a word.

Chapter 7 will explore all the angles involved with *loudness*.

A Superfine Voice is Animated, Expressive, and Well-Pitched.

"Some teachers don't talk in their sleep. They talk in other people's sleep," it's been said.

Who hasn't been turned off by dingy, washed-out voices? Their owners sound as if they'd been injected with embalming fluid.

But monotony isn't a vocal disease that attacks only teachers. It can strike anybody. And unfortunately the drones always suggest to their yawning listeners that they are dreary, wooden bores. If you have no fire in yourself, you can't warm others.

You don't have to be stuffy! Your voice has a marvelous flexibility to stretch up and down. The average voice has a range of twelve to fourteen tones. The vocal wet blanket uses only two to four of these tones!

A too-high pitch can bring you the wrong kind of attention. A lower pitch level is an advantage to both men and women. Dr. Joyce Brothers, a celebrated psychologist, writes, "While pitch is probably more important in a woman's rise up the ladder of success, a male with a very high voice is going to have trouble being taken seriously. A high, thin voice is a distinct disadvantage to a man."

Michael Jackson is great as long as he just sings.

Do you sound dry as a bone, dead as a doornail? Is your voice pitched somewhere in the upper levels of the stratosphere? You need vocal pizazz and pitch placement. Sneak a peek into Chapter 8, which tells you all you need to know about *variety* and *expressiveness*. You may possibly have more fun with it than with any other chapter in the book.

A Great Voice Doesn't Attract Undue Attention to Itself.

The opposite of mumbling and garbling is using arty speech. Articulation that is too labored and false stands out like a zit on the end of someone's nose. The speaker uses certain uncommon pronunciations to achieve elegance.

You're being arty if you talk about your *Aunt Jane* instead of your *Ant Jane*. You're being arty if you start out with to-may-toes in your garden and wind up with cream of to-maw-to soup in your dining room.

ACCENT? WHO, ME?

You probably have one. Actually, a better word is dialect.

If you send a greeting card to your mudda on Mudda's Day, or if you spent your weekend in Long Guyland, you're from New York.

If you sit on a sofar instead of a sofa—you're from Massachusetts.

If you're a boid-watcher instead of a bird-watcher—you're from New Jersey (Joisey?).

If you tell your favorite bartender, "Ah want a bottle of bear"—you're from Texas or Alabama.

If you add a drop of mountain color to right here and come up with ri-cheer—you're from West Virginia or Kentucky.

If you meow when you say how now, brown cow? so that it sounds like heow neow, breown ceow?—you're from Maryland, Delaware, or eastern Pennsylvania.

If you go afishin' instead of fishing—you're from practically anywhere.

You Don't Talk Like Us? You Speak a Dialect with an Accent?

There are three major regional dialects in the United States:

General or standard American is spoken by the greatest number of people in America. Boundary lines between various dialects are not sharp and rigid. In general, however, this dialect is most commonly spoken in the Midwest (as far south as the Mason-Dixon line), in the West, and in parts of the Southwest.

Prominent network newscasters such as Jane Pauley, Tom Brokaw, Dan Rather, and David Hartman use the general American dialect, which is the nationally preferred pronunciation for television and radio speech.

Eastern includes the New England and Middle Atlantic states, although the dialects of New York City, Boston, and Baltimore are touch-and-go and not easy to locate specifically. Compare the speech of certain well-known political leaders from Massachusetts with that of their New York counterparts, and you'll hear vast differences.

Southern is used in the region which is roughly equivalent to the states of the old Confederacy. It extends as far west as Arkansas and into parts of Texas.

Is one of the dialects better than the other two? Definitely not. The educated, cultivated New Yorker can be understood in Nashville just as easily as the cultured Bostonian can be understood in Butte, Montana.

Each of the major dialects has several dozen subdialects. I've personally heard such a simple word as "right" pronounced ten different ways in Dallas—rot and riot representing two of the extremes. A New York cabbie once told me about a friend who had been "killed by a shock ina waduh." Electrical shock? No. A shark. The cabbie was using a subdialect.

We have tapes to prove that former Governor Wallace of Alabama used standard southern dialect when talking to businessmen and college graduates, but with laborers, farmers, and the Ku Klux Klan, he slipped into a folksy subdialect.

No section of the United States has a monopoly on good or correct speech. Nor is there any reason why we should all sound alike any more than we should all look or dress alike. An interesting feature story in a late summer issue of a Fort Worth, Texas newspaper gave advice to Texas preppies about to go to exclusive colleges back east. "Worried about your Texas accent?" asked the writer. "Do not—we repeat—DO *not* attempt to get rid of it. They will absolutely adore it back east."

Where does all of this put you? If you've been told that your dialect is peculiar or quaint or if people complain that it's hard to understand, don't attempt to wipe it out. Simply renovate it. The idea is to sound like the enlightened and educated people in your own area.

Prick Up Your Ears: Listen!

There's a big difference between hearing and listening.

In spite of the fact that we spend thirty percent of each day talking and forty-five percent hearing, most of us don't listen too well. People love to talk but hate to listen.

You're now embarking on a voice improvement program.

An important part of this is learning how to listen carefully and critically to the voices around you. (You can't improve if you have no model to copy but yourself.) Note their bad points as well as their good ones. You won't be too surprised to discover that you share some of their vocal weaknesses, as well as their virtues. You'll soon become more sensitive to your own voice personality. *The first step to improvement is self-awareness.*

You can have some fun with the following exercises, although what I'm asking you to do is tricky—almost impossible. *Do not concentrate on* what *your subject is saying. Concentrate on* how *the subject is saying it.* Become a human sponge. Absorb and size up every sound you hear.

1. Listen to a radio drama, or try this entertaining experiment! Listen to a TV soap opera—preferably one with which you're not familiar—*by closing your eyes* or *keeping the picture off the screen.* Concentrate intensely on the sounds of the voices rather than the dialogue. Many soaps have stereotypes: the "heavy," the Good Samaritan, the "other woman," the decent and long-suffering spouse. Can you identify them by their vocal traits? Do you like or dislike them? Why?

    (Note: For Exercises 2, 3, or 4, consult Checklist A in this chapter. It'll help you!)
2. Again, *listen to, rather than watch,* other types of programs such as talk shows, "60 Minutes," interviews, and newscasts. Don't prejudge the speakers. Empty your mind of physical images or preconceptions. You don't like Diane Sawyer's hairdo? Forget it. You think Mike Wallace is prejudiced? Skip it. You're enamored of Jane Pauley or Tom Brokaw? Cool it.

    Rate and compare their voices. Why do you react favorably to some and unfavorably to others?
3. Your public library probably has recordings of prominent personalities reading poetry, prose, plays, or speeches. Robert Frost and Sylvia Plath have recorded some of their own

WHY READ THIS BOOK?

poetry. Laurence Olivier, Judith Anderson, Richard Burton, and Orson Welles have done scenes from plays. The voices of John Kennedy, Richard Nixon, Martin Luther King, Jimmy Carter, and Ronald Reagan are also available.

Pick one or more of these people. Listen and appraise.

CHECKLIST A: EVALUATE SOMEBODY ELSE'S VOICE

(Make a photocopy of this page and fill it out.)

	YES	NO	If "no," why not? It is:
QUALITY: Is the voice pleasant?			Breathy ___ Nasal ___ Strident ___ Hoarse ___ Harsh ___ Throaty ___
LOUDNESS: Is the voice easily heard?			Too soft ___ Too loud ___ Unvaried ___
ARTICULATION: Is the speech clear, distinct and accurate?			Generally sluggish ___ Sounds: dropped ___ Added ___ Mangled ___
EXPRESSIVENESS: Is the voice animated, varied and well-pitched?			Generally monotonous ___ Sing-song ___ The pitch is: too high ___ too low ___ The rate is: too fast ___ too slow ___
UNOBTRUSIVENESS AND APPROPRIATENESS: Are the speech and pronunciation natural and generally acceptable?			Arty ___ Contains mispronunciations ___ Is a regional dialect ___

OVERALL EFFECTIVENESS:
   Excellent ___ Good ___ Fair ___ Weak ___
TARGET AREAS: In what aspects of voice and speech is improvement most needed?

4. If you can't find a suitable recording, analyze the voices of:

   a close friend
   an acquaintance you dislike
   a clergyperson
   somebody you know who possesses an unusual voice
   a salesperson

5. Record your own voice.
      Make a sample of your voice on a special tape. Put it away. Then, after you've finished your self-improvement program, make a final recording of the same material. This gives you a fine opportunity to check out the *before* and *after* aspects of your voice. Your overall improvement will astound you.
      You're welcome to make up your own material for the first tape job. But here are three selections that work nicely. They're effective because, among other things, they contain all the sounds of the English language most often found to be troublesome.

> Once there was a prince, and he wanted to marry a real princess. He traveled all around the world to find one, but there was always something wrong. There were princesses enough, but he found it difficult to make out whether they were real ones.
>   One evening a terrible storm came along. Suddenly a knocking was heard at the gate of the prince's castle. It was a princess. But what a sight she was after all that dreadful weather. The water ran down her hair and clothes. And yet she said she was a real princess.
>   "We'll soon find out," thought the old queen, the prince's mother. She went into the bedroom, took all the bedding off the bedstead, and laid a pea at the bottom. Then she took twenty mattresses and

laid them on the pea. On this the princess slept all night. In the morning she was asked how she had slept.

"Terribly!" said the princess. "Heaven only knows what was in that bed. It felt as though a huge rock was under the mattress. I'm black and blue all over."

Nobody but a real princess could be as sensitive as that. So the prince married her, for now he knew that he had a real princess. [Fairy Tale]

When you get a hundred million people watching a single pro football game on television, it shows you that people need something to identify with. Pro football is like atomic warfare. There are no winners, only survivors. The football season is like pain. You forget how terrible it is until it seizes you again. Is it normal to wake up in the morning in a sweat because you can't wait to beat another human's guts out? Every time you win, you're reborn. When you win, nothing hurts. When you lose, you die a little. No one knows what to say in the loser's room. How you play the game is for college boys. When you're playing for money, winning is the only thing that matters. Fewer than three touchdowns is not enough, and more than five is rubbing it in. You're a hero when you win and a bum when you lose. That's the game. They pay their money, and they can boo if they feel like it. Hell, if football were half as complicated as some sportswriters make out it is, quite a few of us would never have been able to make a living at it.

I heard someone say, "Pop music is the hamburger of the day." For me, it's a lot more. Music is the commonest vibration, the people's news broadcast. I would like to study music and find out how we could use it to heal. Half the battle is selling music, not singing it. It's the image, not what you sing. Anyway, the softer you sing, the louder you're heard. Music does things to you whether you like it or not. Fast tempos raise your pulse and blood pressure. Slow music lowers them. You know yourself, music can calm the savage beast. A person can charm a snake with a flute. You place speakers in a jungle with wild animals and play Beethoven, and the animals will come into your camp. In music you have to think with the heart and feel with the brain. On stage I make love to 25,000 people; then I go home alone. Not even boot camp could be as tough as being in rock and roll. The truth is where the truth is, and sometimes it's in the candy store. [Janis Joplin]

Turn on your recorder. Talk. Play back. (Hope for the best and be ready for the worst.)

When you play back, use Checklist B, below.

CHECKLIST B: EVALUATE YOUR OWN VOICE

(Make two photocopies to fill out—one for your listening friend.)

	YES	NO	If "no," why not? It is:
QUALITY: Is my voice pleasant?			Breathy ___ Nasal ___ Strident ___ Hoarse ___ Harsh ___ Throaty ___
LOUDNESS: Is my voice easily heard?			Too soft ___ Too loud ___ Unvaried ___
ARTICULATION: Is my speech clear, distinct and accurate?			Generally sluggish ___ Sounds: dropped ___ Added ___ Mangled ___
EXPRESSIVENESS: Is my voice animated, varied and well-pitched?			Generally monotonous ___ Sing-song ___ The pitch is: too high ___ too low ___ The rate is: too fast ___ too slow ___
UNOBTRUSIVENESS AND APPROPRIATENESS: Are my speech and pronunciation natural and generally acceptable?			Arty ___ Contains mispronunciations ___ Is a regional dialect ___

OVERALL EFFECTIVENESS:
    Excellent ___ Good ___ Fair ___ Weak ___
TARGET AREAS: In what aspects of voice and speech is improvement most needed?

2
Sound Off!

There is nothing simple about saying something simple. For example: "How are you?" Four physical structures are involved: Your lungs are the bellows; your vocal cords are sound generators; your throat is a reflector; your mouth molds the sounds.

INHALE! EXHALE! INHALE!! EXHALE!!

1. You should be able to read this on one breath. Try it.

    A dog is smarter than some people. It wags its tail and not its tongue. No matter which screw in the head is loose, it's the tongue that rattles. Everybody agrees that a loose tongue can lead to a few loose teeth. A bit of advice: Say nothing often. There's much to be said for not saying much. It's better to remain silent and be thought a fool than to open your mouth and remove all doubt. If you don't say it, you won't have to unsay it. You never have to take a dose of your own medicine if you know when to keep your mouth shut.

Flunk? Not to worry.

Work on Exercises 2–13, which are coming up shortly. Then go back and try Exercise 1 again. You'll make it!

Are Your Lungs Lax, Laggard, and Languid?

Have you ever watched a youngster with a temper tantrum throw himself on the floor and threaten to hold his breath until rigor mortis sets in? The best thing for parents to do is walk away. Howling Howard couldn't stop breathing even if he wanted to. Breathing for life is automatic.

Take a deep breath.

You'll notice that your chest seems to expand and lift. What are you doing? You're making your body (and lungs) bigger. Air flows in. Inhalation, in other words. But when you exhale, you make your body smaller in volume. Air flows out.

Let's clear up some misconceptions about breathing:

Your lungs do *not* suck in air. They are not hollow sacks. They more closely resemble sponges. Your lungs *are* actually lazy. They lead an easy life.

GOOD BREATHING DOESN'T RESULT FROM HEAVING YOUR SHOULDERS UP AND DOWN!

Is there any method of breathing which will give you the right kind of control? A lot of gibberish has been written about so-called "diaphragmatic" breathing. It would be impossible to breathe normally without the diaphragm! Actually, it makes more sense to talk about *central* or *deep* breathing.

Probably ninety-five percent of you breathe this way. How about the other five percent?

There is one no-no as far as breathing is concerned.

Look at yourself in a mirror or have a friend check you. Don't say a word for sixty seconds. If you're raising and lowering your collarbones and shoulders as you inhale-exhale, you're guilty of clavicular-shoulder breathing. *This has to go!*

What's bad about clavicular-shoulder breathing?

You've heard people who gasp noisily for breath in the middle of a sentence. These perturbed panters sound as if they are suffering from convulsions.

- Clavicular breathing is much more shallow than central breathing. The movements of the upper chest are too meager to provide an adequate amount of air.
- Clavicular breathers are often forced to use a jerky rhythm because they must stop for breath too often.
- Clavicular breathing creates excessive tension in the upper chest, straining the vocal machinery. A grating, strident voice results.

What's Good About Central or Deep Breathing?

Watch a sleeping baby or a napping dog. Where's the movement—the breathing activity? In the middle of their bodies, not at the top of their chests.

- Deep breathing is healthy and natural.
- If you're a deep breather, you have far better control of your air supply. You won't suffer from gaspitis or spasms. You'll avoid jerky rhythms.
- Deep breathing keeps muscular tension and strain away from your vocal apparatus. Voice improvement invariably results.

A huge majority of professional actors, speakers, singers, and athletes use deep, central breathing. Super speaking voices are rarely found among clavicular breathers.

Here are some exercises that will demonstrate the difference between inferior and superior breathing habits. The chances are that you're not a clavicular breather, but if you are, these exercises will convert you to beneficial deep breathing.

2. Stand comfortably erect. Try each of the two methods of breathing. Deliberately exaggerate movements.

Clavicular-shoulder: Get the feel of raising and lowering your collarbones and shoulders.

> **Deep:** Place your hand below your lower ribs in front. Inhale. Exhale.
>
> Which way seems the more natural to you?

3. Try the two techniques again, but this time repeat these sentences aloud as you're exhaling.

   > We get too soon old and too late smart.
   >
   > The finger that turns the dial rules the air.
   >
   > Rub-a-dub-dub. Three men in a tub. How unsanitary!
   >
   > In real life it takes only one to make a quarrel.
   >
   > You have to adjust your running style when you're running on ice.
   >
   > Why is the place where I want to be so often so far from where I am?

   If you're a deep breather, you're on the right track. Jump to Exercise 9.

   If you're an upper chest breather, Exercises 4–8 will help you get rid of this clumsy, inefficient method.

4. Place your hands on your upper chest with your thumbs aimed at your collarbones. Take a deep breath, and then count from one to ten. If you're aware of any noticeable upward movement of your shoulders, repeat the exercise and deliberately use the pressure of your hands to prevent this kind of movement. Repeat this procedure saying the months of the year: January through December.

5. Sit erect in an armless chair. Grab the bottom of the chair seat firmly. Your shoulders should not be able to rise. Inhale and exhale, concentrating on movements near the midregion of the body.

6. Lie flat on your back. Place your right hand on your ab-

domen and your left hand on the upper part of your chest. Breathe as naturally as possible. You'll notice a slow and regular expansion and contraction of the area under your right hand and very little movement under your left hand.
7. (Not for the faint of heart.) From a standing position, bend over and touch the floor—if you can! All the air should be out of your lungs. Begin to inhale. Concentrate on the column of breath as if it were a light entering your body. Slowly, slowly straighten up, inhaling, the light flooding your chest. As you're doing this, spread your arms up and out. Your lungs are full of air. Now begin to exhale. Move your arms back in, and slowly bend your body forward until your fingertips touch the floor again. Your lungs are empty. Repeat several times.
8. Stand. Place a book against your midregion. Inhale. The expansion in this area should force the book out from $3/4$ to $1\ 1/4$ inches. Exhale. The contraction permits the book to go back in. Get the feel of the action.

As that late, great philosopher, Mae West, said: "It ain't so much what you got—it's what you do with what you got."
How much air you inhale isn't half as important as how you control the air supply—particularly during exhalation, because this is when you talk and make most sounds.
Exercises 9–13 will help you find an effortless and comfortable control of this process.

9. Beginning quietly, hold the sound of ah and let the sound swell in loudness. Don't raise the pitch. Then diminish to a soft tone. Work for steadiness and easy control of tone.
10. An interesting experiment: Hold a small, lighted candle six to eight inches in front of your mouth. Exhale, sustaining an s sound. Now do it with an f sound. Your exhalation must be uniform and constant, so the flame doesn't flicker, and certainly doesn't go out.

11. With the second hand of a watch to guide you, allow yourself approximately thirty-five seconds to count aloud to fifty. Now try it on one breath. (It *can* be done, but don't asphyxiate yourself!)

12. You'll notice that some words are comparatively hissy, noisy and wasteful of breath. The s in six, the th in thirteen, the f in fifty-five, for example, are the culprits, especially if you allow too much breath to escape with them. Exhale frugally. Be a miser. Ration and dole out the breath. Breath mustn't be squandered. Don't allow air to leak out *before* you start to make a sound or word, *between* words or phrases, or *within* a word itself. Now repeat Exercise 11, without the "hissers." You'll increase your count.

13. Be ultraconservative with your breath control, and read each of the following on a single breath. They'll be simple to do—at first!

> Jesse James shot children, but only in fact, not in folklore.
>
> And that's the way it is—and most of the time we hope it isn't.
>
> If you're going to do something tonight that you'll be sorry for tomorrow morning, sleep late.
>
> It pays not to leave a live dragon out of your plans, especially if you happen to live near one.
>
> As the poet said, "Only God can make a tree"— probably because it's so hard to figure out how to get the bark on.
>
> Little boys and girls who don't always tell the truth will probably grow up and become weather forecasters. Our tastes change as we mature.
>
> A college is truly a fountain of knowledge, and a great many of us go there to drink. Some students drink at the fountain of knowledge. Others just gargle.

SOUND OFF!

Americans have two chickens in every pot, two cars in every garage, and two headaches for every aspirin. The average American would drive his car to the bathroom if the door was wide enough.

A cocktail lounge is a half-lit room full of half-lit people. The main trouble with liquor is that it makes you see double and feel single. Liquor will kill germs, but you can't get them to drink it.

The best rule in driving through five o'clock traffic is to try and avoid being a part of the six o'clock news. Statistics show that an average of 39,000 people are killed by gas annually. Sixty inhale it, forty light matches in it, and 38,900 step on it. A light foot on the gas beats two under the grass.

It seems that camels were once imported into the United States in the hope that they would be useful in desert fighting. On hearing the news, an Indian chief persuaded the army to give him one of the sturdy animals as a present for his wife. She was so fat that she had already ruined three horses. Alas, when she was hoisted aboard the new beast she achieved fame as the squaw that broke the camel's back.

There isn't much point in bothering with politics. It's much simpler to go directly into crime. A politician is a person who's got what it takes to take what you've got. Politics is like milking a cow. You can accomplish a lot if you have a little pull. Some Americans refer to Washington as the city of protocol, alcohol, and Geritol. We ought to be thankful that we are living in a country where folks can say what they think without thinking.

Hollywood is the only place in the world where a person can get stabbed in the back while climbing a ladder. Two of the cruelest, most primitive punishments Tinseltown deals out to has-beens are the empty mailbox and the silent telephone. They've great respect for the dead but none for the living. And the final product? Ninety-five percent of the movies produced in Hollywood are so dull and stupid that it's preposterous to review them in any publication not intended to be read while chewing bubble gum. Hollywood is one big whore. One good thing about radio. It never shows old movies.

Now go back to Exercise 1, near the beginning of this chapter. You'll have no difficulty reading the 109 words on one breath.

ARE YOU STRETCHED TIGHT?

If you answer YES to any of the following, you probably are.

Are You Worried or Under Pressure Because of . . .

deadlines, datelines, hotlines,
    finances, friends, family problems, fitness,
        love life, looks, livelihood,
            bosses or bombs, teachers or taxes?

I can't do anything about the lurking dangers of ICBMs or the IRS, but I can help you learn how to relax and overcome some of the stress and strain.

Tension and stress are not only enemies of good health, they can also seriously interfere with your resonance and vocal quality. The Wrought-Up Robertas and the High-Strung Hirams of the world produce voices to match—undesirable and displeasing.

If you have a tight, constricted throat with rigid walls, for example, your voice may be strident, jarring, and rasping.

Openness of throat and relaxation of the walls and surfaces will promote a mellow, velvety, and molasses-rich quality.

RELAX—LET GO COMPLETELY!

It can't be done! If you didn't have some muscular tension, you couldn't walk, talk, or blow your nose. "If everything goes right there is something wrong," as B. F. Skinner, Harvard psychologist, once said. "You must have tension to stay alive." "Let go completely" really means: "Try to get rid of *unessential* tension in those muscles not needed to perform your task."

Part of the difference between the professional and the amateur—be it an Olympic champion or a student of voice—is the ability to distinguish between what tension is necessary and what isn't. You're concerned with eliminating the undue tightness that hampers voice improvement. You're committed to finding the right kind of relaxation. But never confuse relaxation with inertia or laxness. Relaxation is selective, conscious, and controlled.

The large muscles of the body are easier to get at and loosen, and you can't isolate and relax the relatively small muscles of your vocal machinery if these large ones are taut, so it is with these that we begin:

14. Stand. Deliberately tense the larger muscles of your body and then let go. Repeat several times.
15. While you're standing, have somebody raise one of your arms slowly and then release it. There should be no resistance, and your arm should fall limply to the side. Repeat, but this time offer some resistance, keeping the rest of your body relaxed. Gradually relax the resisting arm.
16. Sit. Tighten your body. Then relax, allowing your head to fall forward and your arms to dangle loosely at the sides.
17. Select a quiet, comfortable room and lie face up on a sofa or bed. Loosen tight clothing. Unwind mentally. A background of soft, moody music helps. Or relive a previously serene and soothing experience.

Stretch and yawn. The stretching should be intense, but the yawning gentle.

Purposely stiffen the larger muscles of your body and then let go. Repeat this pattern several times.

Lie on your left side and rotate your right shoulder slowly and tensely. After a few seconds, relax your shoulder and continue to rotate it. Try your left shoulder.

Extend your right arm rigidly into the air. Relax it and then let it fall limply. Try your left arm.

Assume a fetal or a near-fetal position. Bow your head forward, draw your arms and legs in toward your chin. Curl up. Tighten your entire body. Think of yourself as being absolutely compact and not much bigger than a basketball. Hold this tense position for six to eight seconds, then suddenly let your body go limp. Try to feel a wave of relaxation sweeping down from your forehead to your feet. Concentrate on removing any tensions around your forehead, eyes, mouth and jaw, neck, and back.

18. The Yec-c-c-ch! exercise. Stand. Pretend that you've accidentally plunged your arm into a barrel of gunk or slime. (It smells terrible and there are little green things wriggling around in it.) Shake your arm vigorously to get rid of the repulsive stuff. It helps to say "Yec-c-c-ch!" as you do this. Repeat, but this time the slime is on your legs, then your torso, and finally your neck and head.

19. Now that you've removed the crinkles and crimples from the larger muscles, let's do the same for the smaller ones.

These exercises will help you loosen the sound-producing mechanisms:

Stretch your neck forward and downward, tensing your jaw and neck muscles. Let your head drop forward so that your chin touches your chest. Don't raise your shoulders as you move your head slowly to your right shoulder, to the rear, to your left shoulder, and forward to your chest again. Rotate your head in this manner several times, maintaining muscular rigidity and tightness. Now repeat these motions, but this time gradually relax your jaw and neck muscles.

SOUND OFF!

Say the following as though sighing. Stre-e-etch those vowel sounds:
aw-haw-arm-cot-caw-maw-palm-tall-mush-mum-sup

20. This tranquil material will help you get unwound. Read it quietly, calmly, and slowly. Pro-o-o-long the vowels slightly. Concentrate on a general feeling of unbending and easing up.

> When it is dark enough, you can see the stars.
>
> What is life? It is the flash of a firefly in the night.
>
> Death tugs at my ear and says: "Live, I am coming."
>
> The Arctic expresses the sum of all wisdom: silence.
>
> Soft heads do more harm than soft muscles.
>
> Even if this is the dawn of a bright new world, most of us are still in the dark.
>
> If I must die I will encounter darkness as a bride and hug it in my arms.
>
> When you are deeply absorbed in what you are doing, time gives itself to you like a warm and willing lover.
>
> Whatever befalls the earth befalls the sons of earth. Man did not weave the web of life. He is merely a strand in it. Whatever he does to the web, he does to himself.

3
Put Your Best Voice Forward!

There is only one voice in the world exactly like your voice—your own. Your voice is you. Most courts of law are now considering voiceprints as acceptable as fingerprints for identifying individuals.

IS YOUR VOICE PLEASANT TO LISTEN TO?

Your voice tells a lot about you. It's a key to your identity. It's your calling card, your trademark, your personal logo.

HOW DO YOU DEVELOP A DESIRABLE VOCAL QUALITY?

General, overall bodily relaxation is the first step, and we've worked on that. But now let's become more specific. Before you can build a winning and charismatic quality—

- Your throat and mouth passageways must be open, relaxed and free of unnecessary tension.
- Your lips, jaw, and tongue must be agile and flexible.
- Tone must be projected to the front of the mouth.

PUT YOUR BEST VOICE FORWARD!

Thaw out your throat and mouth passageways:

1. "Freeze" or tense your throat and jaw muscles and then swallow. Holding this extreme tension for a few seconds, say ah. What happens to your vocal quality?
2. Now, for contrast, relax the jaw and yawn gently as you inhale. With the same degree of ease, say ah. Notice the difference?
3. Keeping the feeling of ease and openness, say these words as though sighing:

how	saw	too	arm
awl	odd	call	cod
coo	mush	sum	aunt
now	shawl	loll	dot

4. Let your jaw remain open and as motionless as possible, and keep the tip of your tongue behind your lower front teeth as you say:

yah-yah-yah-yah-yah-yah-yah-yah
yoh-yoh-yoh-yoh-yoh-yoh-yoh-yoh
yah-you-yoh-yea-hah-hoo-hoh-hey

5. Expa-a-a-nd your vowels slightly as you read these with an open and relaxed throat:

Come up into the hills, O my young love.

Darkness melted over the town like dew.

The hush of dawn washed the murmuring brook in glowing pink.

The quiet music of the stars nudged the heavy clouds of night.

HOW TO SOUND LIKE A MILLION DOLLARS

> The mountains were said to be in labor, and uttered the most dreadful groans. People came together from far and near to see what birth would be produced; and, after they had waited a considerable time in expectation, out crept a mouse.
>
> [Aesop]

> My beloved speaks, and says unto me, Rise up, my love, my fair one, and come away. For, lo, the winter is past, the rain is over and gone; the flowers appear on the earth; the time of the singing of birds is come, and the voice of the turtle is heard in our land. The fig tree putteth forth her green figs, and the vines with tender grapes give a good smell. Arise, my love, my fair one, and come away.
>
> [The Song of Solomon]

Liberate your lips:

6. Open your mouth as widely as you can on the initial sound in each word.

opera	owl	always	army
awful	oddly	ouster	ostrich
almond	otter	office	auk
auger	oxen	alder	ought

7. Give these a snappy reading, exaggerating your lip movements:

   we-we-we-we-we-we-we-we
   re-re-re-re-re-re-re-re
   woo-woo-woo-woo-woo-woo-woo-woo
   waw-waw-waw-waw-waw-waw-waw-waw

8. Overdo mouth opening, jaw activity, and lip agility as you read these:

   Jaw-jaw is better than war-war.

PUT YOUR BEST VOICE FORWARD!

If your cup runneth over, let someone else runneth your car.

The only walk more expensive than a walk down a church aisle is a walk down a supermarket aisle.

Traffic warning sign: "Heads you win—cocktails you lose."

A watched pot often causes one to join weight watchers.

One of the major problems we face each summer is how to get the watermelon into the refrigerator without taking the beer cans out.

Focus the tone forward to the front:

"Bounce your voice off the back wall of the room."
—*impossible!*

You absolutely can't focus or bounce your voice—from a purely scientific point of view. For that matter, ventriloquists don't "throw" their voices either.

On the other hand, these words aren't just gimmicks. If you're told to focus, bounce, or project your voice, you'll respond by opening your mouth somewhat wider than you normally do. Your general articulation will also become more energetic and nimble. As you sharpen up with the material below, direct and aim your tones forward against your upper front teeth. This kind of practicing will give you greater clarity and brilliance of quality.

9. Chant these, but give the oh and aw sounds the same frontal placement and luster of ee:

ee-ee-ee-ee	wee-woh-waw	lee-loh-law
oh-oh-oh-oh	mee-moh-maw	bee-boh-baw
aw-aw-aw-aw	tee-toh-taw	dee-doh-daw

10. Can you carry over the forward placement and brightness of tone from the first sentence to the second and third

sentences of each of these groups? Keep your throat relaxed. Build up the vowel tones, but avoid any hint of hardness or scratchiness.

What we really need in this country is a car that eats oats.
People who row the boat generally don't have time to rock it.
Once you get a reputation as an early riser, you can sleep till noon.
Please drive carefully—the IRS needs you.
If you want to forget all your other troubles, wear shoes that pinch.
A virgin forest is a forest in which the hand of man has never set foot.
When people agree with me, I always feel I must be wrong.
I'm not O.K., you're not O.K., and that's O.K.
Sign on a church lawn: "Keep off the grass. This means thou."

If preachers preach and teachers teach, why don't we say that speakers speech?
The more I know the more I know I don't know.
Love conquers all things except poverty and toothache.

I would rather eat than fish, particularly eat fish.
What you don't see with your eyes, don't invent with your mouth.
There will be prayer in public schools, law or no law, as long as there are final exams.

FEND OFF THE FROTH (BREATHINESS); REMOVE THE RASP (STRIDENCY); SACK THE SCRATCH (HARSHNESS); WIPE OUT THE WHINE (NASALITY); GROUND THE

GROWL (THROATINESS); CURB THE CROAK (HOARSENESS)!!!

Here are seven descriptive terms widely used by voice experts (and you'll remember reading about them earlier in the book):

breathy   denasal
strident   throaty
harsh   hoarse
nasal

Once again, tape your voice or play back something you've already recorded.

Let's face it: Your ears will hear exactly what you want them to hear. A second listener—an umpire—is needed. Give him or her a list of the seven descriptive terms. Ask him or her to make some straight-from-the-shoulder comments about the caliber of your voice.

If it's determined that you have a breathy or a harsh voice—or any of the other qualities I've just listed—

FIND THE APPROPRIATE SECTION IN THIS CHAPTER, AND GET TO WORK!

You may not have a problem of quality. If you don't—lucky you! Move on to the next chapter.

> If you have a quality defect, selected exercises below will help you correct it. *In the unlikely event that you become aware of any vocal strain or discomfort, seek professional help.*

Do You Sound Fuzzy, Whispery, or Feather-Edged? You're Breathy!

If you have a woolly quality, it's because when you're talking, you don't bring your vocal cords together closely enough and unused air leaks between them.

Breathiness is less common among male voices, although many actors in soap operas, particularly in the steamier scenes, tend to produce voices that contain more soap suds than clear and solid tones.

A breathy voice isn't always unattractive. You've noticed how often TV and movie actresses cultivate this vocal cloudiness. Diane Keaton, Bo Derek, Zsa Zsa Gabor, and Goldie Hawn have a smoggy quality. It allegedly makes the voice sound sexy, and some members of the male sex claim to be stirred up by this type of downy charm.

A breathy, wispy voice, however, is often weak and inefficient. Without a mike, it simply doesn't carry. It's monotonous, and may also ticket its owner as extremely shy or sluggish. What's more, breathiness suggests to the world that the foggy-voiced one is not only dim and spineless but also sickly.

The answer is to get just the right amount of tension in your vocal cords. They should be neither too tight nor too relaxed. Don't try to be as limp and floppy as the Scarecrow of Oz. Inadequate tension may be responsible for the failure to bring the vocal cords together completely during tone production. Be aware of muscle adjustments in your throat. Exercises 11, 12, and 13 will help you.

11. Sit like a robot in an armless chair. Grip the sides of the chair and tighten your body, especially your arms and shoulders. Say the pronoun I half a dozen times, using a strong voice. You'll feel some pressure in your throat and hear a firmer tone quality. Then substitute these sentences for I:

> Behind every great man is a woman. Behind her is his wife.

> The family that stays together probably has only one car.

> Soup should be seen and not heard.

Facts do not change; feelings do.

Never slap a man who is chewing tobacco.

12. Stand erect. Extend your arms rigidly in front of you. Hold a fairly heavy book in your hands. Say I several times, and then repeat the short sentences in Exercise 11.
13. Remember Samson of Biblical fame? Stand in an open door with the palms of your hands placed flat against each side of the door. Push as firmly as you can. You'll feel the increased tension of muscles in the abdominal and chest areas. Hold the position for five to six seconds (your vocal folds should now be closed), then release the pressure. Relax. Repeat the "Samson" exercise half a dozen times.

    Repeat, but as you let go, count from one to ten. Make the numbers hard and robust. Do this several times.

    As soon as your voice sounds strong and sturdy with the numbers, try these:

    Do it now! Today will be yesterday tomorrow.

    Blind dates are better than no dates at all.

    God defend me from myself.

    Think twice before you say nothing.

    Never strike a child. You might miss and hurt yourself.

14. As you rehearse the first line in each trio, exaggerate and use a breathy, smoky, and sighing quality. Make the second line louder, and eliminate *some* of the featheriness. The third line should be spoken in a bold voice. Do away with all traces of fuzz and fluff.

    The more the change, the more it is the same thing.
    Beware the fury of a patient person.

I'm an instant star. Just add water and stir.
[Barbra Streisand]

A nose that can see is worth two that sniff.

Saint: a dead sinner revised and edited.

If love makes the world go around, why are we going into outer space?

Man will always delight in a woman whose voice is lined with velvet.

How awful to reflect that what people say of us is true.

The world is getting better every day—then worse again in the evening.

Some people speak from experience. Others—from experience—don't speak.

If you're there before it's over, you're on time.

A good rooster crows in any henhouse.

Energy is beauty. A Rolls-Royce with an empty tank doesn't run.

What is not good for the hive is not good for the bee.

Fun is like life insurance: The older you get, the more it costs.

15. Certain consonants are breathier and hissier than others: s, f, th, h, sh, and p. They're simply molded puffs of air. The problem arises if an individual carries over the hissy sound to a next-door vowel or consonant. In the word shall, for example, the feathery quality of sh shouldn't color the rest of the word:—all. Try doing it the wrong way: Expand the sounds from the above group in these words:

say	should	pop
hill	her	sham
fad	fine	thin
thick	sick	sell

16. This time, cut short each sound with a diagonal line. Don't draw it out.

PUT YOUR BEST VOICE FORWARD!

s̸ay   s̸hould   p̸op̸
h̸ill   h̸er   s̸ham
f̸ad   f̸ine   t̸hin
t̸hick   s̸ick   s̸ell

17. Hold these sounds by beginning with a quiet but non-breathy tone and increasing the loudness of each:

    ah   oh   ee   oo   uh

18. Use full volume as you start these selections, but after you've read a line or two, gradually reduce the loudness until you hit a moderate level of volume that is free of breathiness.

>   It's no secret that organized crime in this country takes in over fifty million dollars a year. This is quite a nice profit, especially when you consider that the Mafia spends very little for office supplies.
>
>   How come it's always the loudest snorer who falls asleep first? A woman can cure her husband's snoring by kindness, patience—or stuffing an old sock in his mouth.
>
>   It's said of Jane Austen that on her deathbed she made it plain that she wanted to say something, and what she wanted to say was that she had written that life was ninety-nine percent chance and she wished to correct this figure to one hundred percent.
>
>   It's surprising how easy it is to tolerate people when you don't really have to. Always be tolerant with a person who disagrees with you. After all, he has a right to his ridiculous opinions.
>
>   The boy called out, "Wolf, Wolf!" and the villagers came out to help him. A few days afterward he tried the same trick, and again they came to his

aid. Shortly after this a wolf actually came, but this time the villagers thought the boy was deceiving them again and nobody came to his aid. A liar will not be believed, even when he speaks the truth. [Aesop]

19. Read the following lustily all the way through. Keep out those vocal vapors!

> If truth is beauty, how come people don't have their hair done in the library?
>
> I'm not very keen for doves or hawks. I think we need more owls.
>
> A person of sixty has spent twenty years in bed and over three years eating.
>
> Grow up as soon as you can. The only time you really live fully is from thirty to sixty.
>
> After you hear two eyewitnesses to an automobile accident, you're not so sure about history.
>
> I expect to pass through this world but once. Any good therefore that I can do, or any kindness that I can show to any human being, let me do it now. Let me not defer or neglect it, for I shall not pass this way again.

Do You Sound Brassy, Piercing or Strained? You're STRIDENT

A popular women's magazine polls its readers yearly. In a recent poll, these were the ten most admired living women:

Queen Elizabeth
Nancy Reagan
Mother Theresa
Geraldine Ferraro
Carol Burnett

Princess Diana
Margaret Thatcher
Barbara Jordan
Sandra Day O'Connor
Ann Landers

Tenth on the list, Ann Landers, is the widely read and popular columnist who dispenses commonsensical and often humorous advice on everything from heartbreak to herpes, paranoia to petting and, occasionally, how to make meat loaf.

It comes as a bit of a shock to some of her fans to hear the lady in person. Hers is an astringent and quite scratchy voice. (It comes as no shock to her. She is aware of it.)

Breathy voices don't always faze hearers, but listening to strident voices is something like having a root canal job without novocaine. It's ear-splitting, steely, and forced. We often associate this sharp and tart kind of voice with a high-strung, jittery, and hypertense individual. (If you're persistently strident, you may have a psychological problem. In this case, professional counseling is recommended.)

Does your voice sound blaring and abrasive even when you're not waspish or up-tight? You can often *see* stridency! Talk to your mirror. Do the veins and muscles in your neck seem to knot or bulge? If they do, your voice may have all the raucous charm of an outraged parrot.

This high-pitched harshness generally results from *excessive* muscular tension in the throat. It's far more characteristic of women's voices than men's, although there are males whose voices have a cawing crow quality.

Stridency is related to one or a combination of several factors:

- Using too much of the wrong kind of loudness.
- Squeezing and rasping the tone out of the throat with no

feeling of bodily support for it. How do you get that body support? Chapter 7 will tell you.
- Shallow breathing. Have you checked your breathing recently? Remember, clavicular breathing promotes tension in the throat. Deep breathing doesn't. If you need to, check Exercises 2–8 in Chapter 2.
- Unnaturally tight throat. Review Exercises 19 and 20 in Chapter 2.

20. Locate the V-shaped notch at the top of your Adam's apple. Say this sentence several times at a comfortably low pitch level:

    She and he weeded the wiry seaweed.

    If you can't find the notch, you may be raising your larynx too high in your throat. Again, too much tension is the villain. Practice until you're able to lower the larynx to its normal position.

21. With your tongue on the floor of your mouth, start an easy, gentle yawn. Your throat area is reasonably relaxed. Whisper ah and hold for about five seconds. Gradually add voice to the whisper, and build it up to a moderately loud level. But don't allow a feeling of tightness to creep into your throat. Repeat with these sounds:

    ee (meet) oh ah ow oo (moon) oi uh

22. As you do the first line in each group, *be a tad strident*. (Don't overdo the stridency! A little bit goes a long way.)
    But read the second line with a soft-boiled and hushed quality.

Now, for contrast, try the third line with a normal quality—no stridency, no hush-hush.

>(strident) The wheel that squeaks the loudest is the one that gets the grease.
>(breathy) Conscience is the inner voice which warns us that someone may be looking.
>(normal) Hit the ball over the fence, and you can take your time going around the bases.

>(strident) "Be yourself!" is about the worst advice you can give some people.
>(breathy) People don't change. They just become more so.
>(normal) A hole is nothing at all, but you can break your neck in it.

>(strident) It doesn't matter if you're rich or poor, as long as you've got money.
>(breathy) If your soul is in your belly, nobody can drive you out of your skull.
>(normal) Everything comes to one who waits—among other things, death.

>(strident) If an atom bomb destroys the human race, will surviving turtles wear people-neck sweaters?
>(breathy) It's hard for an empty bag to stand upright.
>(normal) Don't borrow trouble. Borrow money, and trouble will come of its own accord.

>(strident) A newscast always starts off with "Good evening"—and then proceeds to tell you why it isn't.
>(breathy) Many motorists tend to drive much too close to the cars behind them.
>(normal) If we all obeyed the Ten Commandments, there'd be no "Ten O'Clock News," would there?

23. Deliver these in a leisurely manner and stre-e-e-tch your vowel sounds. Pay careful attention to breathing and pitch

level. Work for proper relaxation, and unconstricted throat, and, of course, a vocal quality that is not caustic or strident.

Faith is the bird that feels the light when the dawn is still dark.

I would rather sit on a pumpkin and have it all to myself than be crowded on a velvet cushion.

Let us be silent that we may hear the whispers of the gods.

Death comes like a thief in the night. Don't let yourself get mugged.

The trouble with being poor is that it takes up all of your time.

The wild places are where we began. When they end, so will we.

Do You Sound Rough, Raspy, Grunty, and Growly? You're HARSH!

This type of voice is gruff, husky, and guttural. No pun is intended, but guttural is a fine choice of word, because a scraping voice seems to grind its way up from a vocal gutter.

A harsh voice is invariably low-pitched. In a sense, then— *what strident is to the female voice, harsh is to the male voice.*

The owners of these corrosive voices sometimes create the impression that they're cold and unsympathetic individuals, if not downright "meanies." Movie and TV toughs or heavies like Orson Welles, Jack Nicholson, Charles Bronson, and Robert Mitchum make use of voices like human hacksaws as a way to create their tough-guy characterizations.

John Houseman took advantage of a grainy and shaggy voice to create the iron-hard old law professor in *The Paper Chase*. He's also made a few millions with TV commercials. Says he: "They've made me into a crusty old household word."

What causes harshness?

- Not enough energy in your speech. Many people with harsh voices have improved substantially by speaking more energetically. Need more zeal and zest? Peek ahead into Chapter 7, Exercises 1–8.
- Permitting your tongue to hump up in your throat. Pulling back the tongue muffles the tone and also contributes to mealy-mouthed articulation.
- Burying your chin in your neck while speaking. If you do this (once again, have a dialogue with a mirror and check that chin position), you're pulling the voice box down into an abnormally low position.
- Too much relaxation of the throat.
- Too much tension in the throat area. Review Exercises 1–5 in this chapter.

If you're still harsh, Exercises 24–27 will set you on the right course.

24. RAGGEDY ANN—RAGGEDY ANDY Be a rag doll and lower the upper part of your body so that your shoulders almost rest on your knees. Let your head flop around and your arms dangle loosely at the sides. Do you feel comfortably relaxed?

    Now sit up, but keep the same easy relaxed feeling that you had a second ago.

25. Do a rerun on Exercise 24, but this time, while in the sitting up phase, hum n quietly. Hum on various pitches, taking a breath between each change of pitch, holding the hum for five to ten seconds.

26. Repeat the humming, but now do it louder and with more relish. Contrast and compare what you did in the previous exercise with what you're doing now. Can you *feel* a difference?

27. Lower your pitch a tone or two as you speak the first line in each group. Let the words fall back into your throat, and speak with as little gusto as possible. Be exhausted! You'll find yourself simulating a grating, growly quality.

The second line: Raise your pitch one or two tones and read in a *relatively* strong voice but don't overdo!

The third line: Use a normal quality, with no trace of harshness. Concentrate on the second and third lines in each group.

If you don't feel pain, you don't feel anything, and that's not living.

Etiquette: learning to yawn with your mouth closed.

A critic is one who knows the way but can't drive the car.

An alarm clock is a device that makes you rise and whine.

Kissing a smoker is a little like making love to an ashtray.

For Christmas, why not give the gift that keeps on giving? A female cat.

You're never going to get anywhere if you think you're already there.

Millions of Americans aren't working, but thank heavens they've got jobs.

You're not drunk if you can lie on the floor without hanging on.

If at first you don't succeed—push!

Sign in a liquor store: "Preserve wild life. Throw a party!"

You're making progress if each mistake you make is a new one.

A road sign in Texas: "Drive like hell, and you'll get there."

Blessed are the teenagers, for they shall inherit the national debt.

Carrots are good for the eyes. Have you ever seen a rabbit with glasses?

PUT YOUR BEST VOICE FORWARD!

Do you sound like grease in an over-heated frying pan? You have VOCAL FRY!

Here's an odd vocal foible—an offshoot of harshness—which one hears now and then. You don't have to be consistently harsh to be a victim of the "Irksome Quirk"—as it's so aptly nicknamed. If you drop the pitch of your voice down into the cellar at the end of a phrase or sentence, the final sound is a croak—a noise from the back of the vacuum cleaner. It sounds something like bacon frying.

Sometimes the "fry" has to do with poor breath control. If your air supply is depleted, the last few words of a thought or phrase may be squeezed out of your throat with a popcorn-popping quality.

Tape a short paragraph. When you play back, listen scrupulously to the ends of sentences. If the last few words seem to have that basement buzzsaw rumble, you're a victim of vocal fry.

Here's what you can do about it:

28. Start each of these words on a fairly high pitch, and then slide your voice downward. When you've reached the lowest level that you can—without the crackle—prolong the vowel sound.

maw	who	lay	raw
they	me	do	fee
why	sea	doe	nay
new	low	tea	no

29. Now do the opposite of what you just did in Exercise 28. Slide your voice upward on each word. As you begin, let your voice fall back into your throat and rumble. Raise the pitch slowly, and as soon as you hear and feel the disappearance of the smudgy quality, hold the vowel sound for a few seconds on that particular pitch level.

awe	sow	aunt	ale
plow	all	eel	ear

caught	ow	ore	ire
sought	add	keen	ask

30. The following material is loaded with tongue-tip sounds. These will compel you to push your tongue quite far forward. Aim for sturdy, untarnished sounds. Slightly more forceful projection will also help you eliminate vocal fry.

If I had my life to live over again, I would have eaten less cottage cheese. [Erma Bombeck]

A tax refund is the next best thing to being shot at and missed.

Without red cells, blood would bleed to death.

The devil and me, we don't agree. I hate him, and he hates me.

Some people are like musical glasses: to produce their finest tones, you must keep them wet.

All work and no play makes Jack a dull boy—and Jill a wealthy widow.

Do You Sound Like A Foghorn? Do You Twang or Whine Through Your Nose? You're NASAL!

"A country singer," Dolly Parton said, "is a person who sings through his nose by ear."

Nasality is a loose word. The bottom line: There are two kinds—*too much* and *too little*. First, I'll talk about the *too much* kind.

31. With your thumb and forefinger pinch your nose, closing off your nostrils, and say:

Television is what gives you something to do when you aren't doing anything.

Feel the vibrations in your nose—especially on m, n, and ng?

32. Put a clean mirror in a freezer compartment for a few minutes. Then place it under your nostrils and read the test sentence in Exercise 31 again, not holding your nose. There should be small clouds on the mirror.

33. Once again, pinch your nose and say:

Hollywood's all right. It's the pictures that are bad.

You should feel no vibrations. If you do, you're talking through your nose: You have too much nasality.

34. With a cold, clean mirror re-read the test sentence in Exercise 33, not holding your nose. This time, there should be no cloudy spots on the mirror. If there are—you're nasal.

What causes this excessive nasality?

- Your tongue humps in the rear of your mouth. Sound is blocked from coming out the mouth. It backfires and is directed through your nose.
- Your jaw is too rigid, and your teeth are clenched or nearly closed. The sound gets trapped in your throat.
- Dilapidated articulation and talking too softly *increase* nasality. A wider mouth opening, talking louder, and zippier articulation will help you *decrease* nasality.

Three of our most pleasant and musical sounds are m, n, and ng (as in sing). They're also the only three *legitimate* nasal sounds in the English language.

Want proof? m, n, and ng must be directed through your nose. Hum m for a few seconds and then pinch your nostrils with thumb and forefinger. You'll cut off the sound.

Now sing aw for a few seconds and then pinch your nostrils. It makes no difference. Aw can be produced with the nasal passages closed off.

Remember—as you practice the following—only m, n, and ng are nasally produced. All other sounds are aimed primarily through the mouth.

35. Don't navigate those vowels through your nose!
    Hold aw briefly, pause, and then add the nasal sound. Repeat the process without the pause.

    aw . . . . . m   aw . . . . . n   aw . . . . ng
    awm   awn   awng

    Follow the pattern of the first exercise but place the nasal at the beginning.

    m . . . . aw   n . . . . . aw   ng . . . . aw
    maw   naw   ngaw

    Place the vowel between the nasals.
    m . . . aw . . . m   n . . . aw . . . n   ng . . . aw . . . ng

36. There are no nasal sounds in the first line of each pair below. The second line is saturated with them. Exaggerate the nonnasal quality of the initial sentence, but as you read the second sentence, try to ricochet the tones through your nose. Repeat until you can *feel* and *hear* the differences.

    If you drive a car, I'll tax the street. If you try to sit, I'll tax the seat. [George Harrison]
    A censor is a person who knows more than he thinks you ought to.

    Whoever gossips to you will gossip about you.
    One reason I don't drink is that I want to know when I'm having a good time. [Brooke Shields]

PUT YOUR BEST VOICE FORWARD!

I have a perfect cure for a sore throat. Cut it.
[Alfred Hitchcock]
Don't be so humble. You're not that wonderful.
[Golda Meir]

Death is a very soft word.
I base most of my fashion taste on what doesn't itch. [Phyllis Diller]

Politics is like football. If you see daylight, go through the hole.

Other people's sins are before our eyes; our own are behind our back.

37. These sentences have no nasals. Do each one twice, first in the ordinary way and then while pinching off your nostrils. There should be no appreciable difference in the sound of the two sentences. If there is and if you feel a prickly commotion in your nose, you're probably too nasal. Wider mouth opening and perky articulation will help you.

The best way out is always through.

To teach is to touch a life forever.

Death is the greatest kick of all. That's why they save it for last.

School days could be the happiest days of your life—if your kids are of the right age to go.

Zoo: a great place to study the habits of people.

Tact is to lie to others as you would have others lie to you.

38. Watch those nosy nasal neighbors!

Pronounce: nan and lap

You'll notice that the vowel a is more nasal in nan than it is in lap. The three nasals, m, n, and ng have a tendency to

HOW TO SOUND LIKE A MILLION DOLLARS

carry over and strongly affect neighboring vowels. Too much of this can give your voice a nasal aura.

Read the following word pairs. Words to the left contain no nasals. Words to the right do. Stress or round out the vowels and hang onto the nasals briefly. But be careful not to jump the gun by allowing the vowels to become nasal.

fat–Nat   Ed–end   yet–net
tip–nip   big–bin   code–node
row–no   lake–lane   Vic–vim

39. The first time you say these words, overdo the nasal sounds. The second time, avoid overdoing. Be sure that there's no nasal spill.

ma'am   moat   next   mate
mantle   nil   mouse   mask
nag   banned   mouth   mitt

40. Overplay the nasal quality the first time you read the following. Repeat, but avoid the nasality that lingers from a nearby m, n, or ng.

> I'd leave a man for a movie, but I'd never leave a movie for a man. [Elizabeth Taylor]

> There are moments when everything goes well. Don't be frightened. It won't last.

> Never eat anything at one sitting that you can't lift. [Miss Piggy]

> When angry, count to ten. When very angry, swear. [Mark Twain]

We cannot unthink unless we are insane.

When one burns one's bridges behind one, what a nice fire it makes!

Do you sound stuffy, cold-in-the-headish, dehydrated? You're Denasal.

There are two kinds of nasality—*too much* and *too little*, also known as denasality.

"Good bawdig. Sprig has cub, ad I have a bad cold id by dose."

Ever sound like that? Your case of sniffles is temporary, of course, but once in awhile we hear a voice which always sounds blocked and congested.

Sylvester Stallone, in his Rocky movies, deliberately worked for the broken-nose, bottleneck effect. That's great for playing a punch-drunk boxer. Otherwise, denasality can seriously hamper understandability of speech.

Denasality happens if a small amount of air or no air at all enters the nasal passages as you talk. Sometimes a barrier is responsible: Enlarged adenoids, swollen tonsils, hay fever, or a broken nose will give you this nasal roadblock.

Possibly, surgical repair or medical treatment is needed. Unfortunately, even after such treatment, some individuals remain denasal. A little vocal retraining will generally solve the problem.

41. Hum m, n, and ng (as in ring) up and down the scale. You'll feel vibrations and tinglings on your lips and in your nasal passages.
42. You won't feel any ripples in your nose as you say the first word in each pair below. But as you say the second word, prolong m, n, and ng, and you'll feel prickling sensations there.

bay–May	dell–Nell	bag–bang
bad–mad	day–nay	run–rung
bail–mail	dill–nil	big–bing

43. Run through the following words twice, the first time slowly and the second time rapidly. In both readings, make the nasal sounds as prominent as you can.

an	lime	noon	moll
sign	bone	mat	bend
aunt	rhyme	moon	chin

44. Speak each of the sentences below twice. The first time stretch the nasal sounds so that you're definitely aware of nasal tremors. Work up to an eight on the Richter scale. Can you make the tone quality of the vowels and diphthongs as vibrant and ringing as it is on m, n, and ng?

    The second time, don't exaggerate, but be certain that m, n, and ng have normal nasality and that your vowels and diphthongs also have a bit of luster.

   Today if you invent a better mousetrap, the government comes along with a better mouse. [Ronald Reagan]

   May the fleas of a thousand camels infest your armpits. [Arab curse]

   Some are bent with toil, and some get crooked trying to avoid it.

   Classical music is the kind that we keep thinking will turn into a tune.

   In about twenty years today's trying times will have become the "good old days."

> The best thing about movies: You're giving people little, tiny pieces of time that they'll never forget.
> [Paul Newman]

Do You Sound Muffled, Trapped, Zombie-Like? You're THROATY!

This is a "voice-from-the-tomb" quality—a heavy echo bouncing off the back wall of a cave. It almost sounds as if its owner has a physical obstacle in the mouth that prevents the voice from coming out.

Not surprisingly, when TV comedy actors want to portray a character as a dummy, a booby, or a nerd, they often use this sooty, throaty quality.

Outside the entertainment world, this dammed-up kind of voice can be objectionable to listeners because it generally lacks carrying power. It sounds swallowed and thick. The peculiar clogged quality attracts attention, if not necessarily approval. (Throatiness has been described as "vocal constipation.")

If you can "see" a strident voice, you can also "see" a throaty voice. The throaty person likes to bury the chin against the neck, and a hollow, voice-in-the-sewer-pipe sound emerges. "Keep your chin up," in other words, is fine advice in more ways than one. *Check your chin position* in a mirror.

45. Do these minisentences three times: The first time, pull your chin back against your neck.

    The second time, go to the other extreme. Tilt your head back quite far, and raise your chin high.

    The third time, strike a compromise posture. Your chin should be in a normal position. Your throatiness should disappear. If you're still having problems, repeat the techniques suggested for the second and third readings, but omit the first, chin-against-the-neck position.

One thing this country needs is fewer needs.

A penny saved is a penny taxed.

A slap on the back often pushes out the chest.

Always give the public what they want, even if they don't want it.

On, no! Not nuclear war! What about my career?

Don't pray for rain if you're going to complain about the mud.

46. Is your tongue position correct?
If your tongue is consistently pulled too far back or humped up toward the rear of your mouth, certain of your important vowel sounds will be murky and inky. Try the sentences below three different ways:

First, retract your tongue. Pull it *as far back as you can*, and read the sentence. You'll notice that some of the sounds will be greatly distorted.

Second, move your tongue *slightly forward* as you read.

Finally, push your tongue *far forward*. Definitely get the feeling that most of the activity involves the front part of your tongue.

It is easy for eager eagles to eat eels.

She dipped the sheep meat into the stream.

The imp bit the knit mitt.

Stand still and watch the world go by—and it will.

Fame is all right if you don't inhale.

We don't all think alike. In fact, we don't all think.

47. The first sentence in these pairs is chock-full of sounds that have warmth and sparkle—front vowels and tongue-

PUT YOUR BEST VOICE FORWARD!

tip consonants. You'll find it easy to avoid throatiness while reading this material.

The second sentence in each pair is studded with dark and dusty sounds—sounds that lack sheen.

Try to transfer at least some of the brightness and the feeling of the front-of-the-mouth production that you had with the first sentence. Repeat the exercises until you're able to read all of the material with a luminous quality.

Deed: past tense of do. "Macbeth deed the bloody did."
Never trouble trouble till trouble troubles you.

The first and greatest commandment: Don't let them scare you.
A budget tells us what we can't afford, but it doesn't keep us from buying it.

Rain is much nicer than snow because you don't have rain plows piling up rain in eight-foot piles.
If God wanted us to be brave, why did He give us legs?

Middle age is when you're sitting home on Saturday night and the telephone rings and you hope it isn't for you.
Stars in which one no longer believes grow pale.

Tax reform: When you take the taxes off things that have been taxed in the past and put taxes on things that haven't been taxed before.
Prayer of the modern American: "Dear God, I pray for patience, and I want it right now."

Washing your car and polishing it all up is a never-failing sign of rain.
It is better to be hated for what you are than loved for what you are not.

Do You Sound Rusty and Rasping? You're HOARSE!

This is the Gravel Gerty and Gravel Gordy voice. It's raw. It's rough and gruff. Hoarse people don't talk—they croak!

Hoarseness due to a bad cold or sore throat will disappear when the cold goes away. Chronic hoarseness, however, is dangerous—it's like committing vocal suicide.

> If your voice is affected by chronic hoarseness, see a physician!

Persistent hoarseness may result from nodes or polyps (noncancerous growths, something like small knobs, on the vocal cords). Malignant tumors are also responsible for trouble. Surgical treatment is generally required for these more serious defects.

What causes these growths? Vocal abuse is often responsible.

- Like to yell a lot at baseball or football games? This is vocal violence at its worst. Screamers' nodes may result.
- Prolonged or excessive loud talking is another probable cause. Actors, both amateur and professional, occasionally lose their voices because of this.

After you've been checked out, and any pathological condition ruled out or corrected, you'll be ready for a program of retraining your voice. A period of vocal rest is often prescribed. This means complete vocal silence—several days to several months. A brilliant operatic soprano, Lucretia Bori, finding herself with chronic hoarseness, refrained from talking or singing for an entire year! Even whispering must be eliminated. Smoking, of course, is also taboo. (A hoarse voice is often called a "smoker's voice"—even if its owner is a nonsmoker.)

If your hoarseness has been brought under control and you're ready for vocal renovating, these exercises will help you:

In Chapter 2—exercises for relaxation, 14–20.
In this chapter—exercises for relaxation, 1–5.
                exercises for harshness, 24–27.
In Chapter 7—exercises for loudness and pitch level, 5–8.

4
Conserve Your Consonants

WHUJUSAY?

Joe and Ed in this scene are not rejects from *Invasion of the Body Snatchers*. They're from Zap, North Dakota, and one of them is a fisherman. Can you translate?

JOE: Hiyed.
ED: Lojo. Whatimes zit?
JOE: Boutaquar nine.
ED: Whujusay?
JOE: Quarnine. Howzt gon?
ED: Nasaha.
JOE: Whutsamatta?
ED: Jescopla bites.
JOE: Gonexra beer?
ED: Godaball Beefeargin. Wanna snor?
JOE: Nah. Godago.
ED: Wazzarush?
JOE: Gotpoinmen adenis. See yamorrow.
ED: Takedezy.
JOE: Guluk!

Joe and Ed are afflicted with a tiresome and commonplace verbal disease: furry and slurry speech—poor articulation. How did the gentlemen get this way?

Laziness? Apathy? Nervous tension, problems of health and hearing, of course, contribute to gummy, dilapidated speech. What about environment? If Joe and Ed's parents, their playmates, their teachers, have contaminated speech, it tells us why Joe and Ed mutilate their speech.

ARE YOU A MUMBLER?

If your speech is mushy and slushy, it won't be easy to convince you that your articulation needs overhauling.

The worst mumbler I've ever known, a computer specialist, once said to me: "Mebbe issa condence, but se'ral m'bes frens seem tabe gittin deaf. I dunno whasamatta. They kin ne'er unerstan anathin I sayn keep askin me ta r'peat alla time."

He had never heard his recorded voice. I taped him. When we played it back, at first he was aghast, then furious. Mr. Mumbles accused me of either hexing his tape or sneaking in somebody else's voice!

I arranged for two of his friends to be present as witnesses and then taped him again. It took the three of us to persuade him that what he heard was truly himself. He decided to take some action, and in a few weeks tidied up his articulation.

> *About three people in one hundred have good or superior articulation. More than one-third speak so indistinctly that they are in need of some kind of special help.*

Startling? Yes, indeed—in view of the fact that at least ninety percent of all the communicating we do is oral! And all listeners like to hear sharp and crisp sounds, because it obviously makes the job of listening easier. Of course, you can go too far. William Buckley, well-known TV commentator, bothers some people with his highly clipped and glossy articulation. Each syllable shimmers like a sword's blade. His speech suggests snobbishness to many listeners.

Good, impeccable articulation is natural. It avoids either of two extremes: sloppiness and artificiality. Natural articulation is speech that is as clear and sharp-edged as it is unforced and effortless. And your listeners aren't distracted by clotted consonants and voluptuous vowels.

Always bear in mind that you speak most often in phrases and sentences and not in disconnected words. Your language tends to flow along smoothly. It's fluid and supple. Words seemingly melt or blend into one another.

Would you really say at lunch, for example: (Pause where you see the double vertical lines).

Please| |pass| |the| |bread| |and| |butter

Probably not. The chances are you'd say:

Pleasepassthebread'n'butter

Overlapping, connected speech isn't a slow-moving, old-fashioned freight train—an open space between each boxcar. Instead, it's a slick Amtrak streamliner.

Overlapping telescopes sounds—reduces the "travel time" between sounds, as it were. It also increases the speed and overall efficiency of articulation. It's easier to say

merry g'round	than	merry		go		round
bustop	than	bus		stop
what ya doing?	than	what		are		you		doing?
black 'n' blue	than	black		and		blue

If overlapping is common and necessary in our speaking, what was wrong with the way Joe and Ed were talking?

These two mumblemouths were carrying overlapping to the nth degree.

If you say "jeat?" instead of "Did you eat?" "fyull" for "if you'll," your overlapping is extreme.

There are more than forty sounds in the English language. Many of them are simple and uncomplicated. A handful are slippery and complex.

Which ones bother you?

You'll enjoy "The Haunted House." Tape it. Note the

underlined consonants—these are often troublemakers and contribute to haphazard and sloppy articulation.

Listen carefully to the tape with your incorruptible friend. If your enunciation seems to need remodeling, don't just shrug your shoulders; fix it! Remember: You may always be intelligible to yourself, but that doesn't mean you're intelligible to others. What's more, you could be totally deaf, and still know what you're *thinking,* so you're not a good judge of how clear you *sound.*

After you've recorded the tale, I'll give you a guide that will tell you specifically what to monitor when you play back.

The Haunted House

[A]   Once upon a **t**ime in a li**tt**le mi**d**wes**t**ern ham**l**e**t**, there was an ol**d** haun**t**ed house. **P**ro**b**a**bl**y **t**wo **d**ozen **p**eo**pl**e had **t**ried **t**o s**t**ay there a**ll** nigh**t**. **B**u**t** before midnigh**t**, they wou**ld** inevita**bl**y **b**e s**c**ared ou**t b**y a frigh**t**fu**l g**host.

Pau**l** Wi**ll**iams, a new **l**o**c**a**l** minister, de**c**i**d**ed **t**o invesi**t**iga**t**e. He wen**t t**o the **d**ark, for**b**i**dd**ing house. He **b**ui**lt** a **g**ood fire, **l**i**t** a **l**am**p**, an**d** sa**t** there rea**d**ing the **B**i**bl**e. Then just **b**efore midnigh**t**, he heard something wa**l**king back and forth in the **b**asement. Everything was **q**uie**t** as a morgue for a few se**c**on**d**s, an**d** then he heard s**t**e**p**s **c**oming u**p** the basement stairs.

[B]   **P**au**l w**atched the doo**r t**o the **c**e**ll**ar. The s**t**e**p**s **w**ere ge**tt**ing **cl**oser an**d l**oude**r**. **Q**uivering **w**ith fright, **P**au**l** ye**ll**ed, "**Who** a**r**e you? **W**ha**t d**o you **w**ant?"

The **gh**astly **cr**eature **w**alked straight toward him. He**r** flesh **w**as d**r**o**pp**ing off he**r** face so that he could see the skull underneath. She had no eyeba**ll**s, but the**r**e **w**as a strange blue light in back of he**r lur**id, **r**ed eyesockets.

[C]   She sta**r**ted **w**ai**l**in**g**. "**My** fiancé and I were **pl**annin**g** a June we**dd**in**g**. **B**u**t** Jonathan **m**u**rd**e**r**ed **m**e fo**r m**y **m**oney, and bu**r**ie**d m**y body **in** the basement." **S**o**bb**in**g** an**d m**oanin**g**, she **c**o**mm**an**d**e**d** hi**m** to take the end joint of the little finger of her left hand and lay it on the collection plate in church next Sunday. He'd find out who her murderer was.

"And then," said the Haunt, "come back to this house. We can meet once more. I will tell you where my money is hidden."

[D]   Next Sunday, the Reverend Williams set the fingerbone in the collection plate. When the brass plate was passed to a man in the last pew, a strange thing took place. Jonathan accidentally touched the fingerbone, and it stuck to his hand. He frantically scraped at the bone. Then he screamed and confessed to the vile murder. They took him to prison.

After Jonathan was executed, Williams returned to the house, and the Haunt's voice told him to dig under the fireplace. He did, and found an enormous chest of silver.

[Folk Tale]

Checklist for The Haunted House

In Section A—the sounds in bold type are *plosives:* t, d, p, b, k, g

Did you . . .

Hack off final plosives—the ends of words? Say ol' for old, lam' for lamp, dar' for dark? Muffle the middles of words? Say pro'ly for probably?

Distort medial t into d? Say liddle for little?

You're blotting out or smothering your plosives. Spend some time with the *plosives,* in this chapter.

In Section B—the sounds in bold type are *glides:* l, r, w

Did you . . .

Swallow the l sounds? Say paw instead of Paul? Queer your r sounds? Make them odd or different enough to cause people to notice them? Wash out or weaken w, especially at the beginnings of words?

CONSERVE YOUR CONSONANTS

You have a leaden tongue and steel lips. Look over *glides,* in this chapter.

In Section C—the sounds in bold type are nasals: **m, n, ng**

Did you . . .

Skimp and scant m and n? Say bas'nt for basement, cameet for can meet?

Heist ng and replace it with an emaciated substitute? Say gettin' for getting, comin' for coming?

Tack a hard g onto an ing? say wedding-g for wedding, sobbing-g for sobbing?

You're nipping and nicking your nasals. Do the section on *nasals,* in this chapter.

In Section D—the underlined sounds are *fricatives:* s, z, th, (as in thin), th (as in the), f, v

Did you . . .

Hiss and whistle s and z sounds?

Blast f and v sounds?

Confuse th (as in thin) with th (as in the)?

Scramble f and v and say file for vile?

Your fricatives are bulging and ruptured. Visit the *fricative family,* in this chapter.

THE ALL-PURPOSE ARTICULATORS

You form and sculpt speech sounds by the movements of your

- . . . **lips**, which pout and protrude, squeeze and stretch, relax and rebound. They *pucker*: weep, wool, oats. They *touch*: pill, beet, man. They *spread*: cheese, he, eel.
- . . . **front teeth**, which help out when your tongue or lower lip touch them. Say: Velma, be very thorough and think this through. You'll feel your lower lip or your tongue tip contact your upper teeth.

> ... **lower jaw**, which opens and closes in varying degrees. Drops on awl and calm, but is almost closed for veal and few.
>
> ... **tongue**, which flattens, flits, narrows, and furrows; stretches and spreads; pushes and pulls.
>
> Ever watch the darting tongue of a chameleon? Your tongue's movements, if not quite as visible, are almost as spectacular. If you say da-da-da as fast as you can, the way a baby might babble, the tip of your tongue is moving about eight times per second!
>
> Notice the variety of tongue positions as you say: think, these, bust, buzz, fool, show, noon, suit.

Let's go back to Ed and Joe. Assuming their organs of articulation are normal, what is it about the articulation itself that makes their speech so flabby and blurred? *Lazy Lips, Jaded Jaw,* and a *Taut Tongue*!!

You've observed and heard the person who speaks with almost limp lips. Ed and Joe are excessively lax- and loose-lipped.

Sports commentator O. J. Simpson, for all his charm and good looks, now and then is guilty of spongy, muddy articulation.

Then you know the speaker who draws his lips into two narrow, iron bands. Invariably, the jaw is also rigid and unmoving. Barbara Walters, another prominent TV personality, has often been accused of speaking with tight lips and a frozen jaw.

Some people learn to speak quite nimbly with a pipe or cigar clenched between the teeth. Others don't even need a prop to do it. This kind of lock-jawed articulation worked well for the late Humphrey Bogart with his ice-cold voice, and it comes in handy for convicts engaged in prison yard talk. For the rest of us, a rusty jaw may strangle the sound. Open your mouth!

CONSERVE YOUR CONSONANTS

Let's Scrimmage!

The San Francisco Forty-Niners don't hold their first practice on Friday and then play the Miami Dolphins on Sunday. Both teams start working out months prior to their first game. A professional soprano spends months—sometimes years—running up and down dreary scales before she finally steps on the stage at the Met and performs. Ballet stars spend hours and hours every week limbering up at the barre. The public sees the finished product—*Swan Lake.*

The exercises in this chapter are some push-ups, scales, and limberer-uppers that will loosen your lips, tongue, and jaw:

How to Keep a Stiff, Upper Lip (Don't)

1. Push your lips out as far as you can, and then pull them back tightly into an extreme smiling position. Repeat several times.
2. Make much of lip movements as you say these:

   too-tee-too-tee-too-tee-too-tee
   too-tay-tee-taw-too-tay-tee-taw
   wee-way-wee-way-wee-way-wee-way

   The one who eats is the one who works.

   Today is the tomorrow you worried about yesterday.

   A man without a wife is like a man in winter without a fur hat. [Russian proverb]

   At a dinner party one should eat wisely, but not too well, and talk well but not too wisely.

   If this is coffee, please bring me some tea. If this is tea, please bring me some coffee. [Lincoln]

How To Jiggle and Joggle Your Jaw

3. Drop your jaw easily as if you were going to say aw. Then move your relaxed jaw from left to right with your hand.
4. Build up jaw movements as you say these:

taw-taw-taw-taw-taw-taw-taw-taw
goo-gaw-goo-gaw-goo-gaw-goo-gaw
gee-gaw-gee-gaw-gee-gaw-gee-gaw

Cars and bars mean stars and scars.

It is awfully difficult for the tolerant to tolerate the intolerant.

Sign in a car on an out-of-the-way parking lot: "Attention, car thieves—this car is already stolen."

The wrong sort of people are always in power because they would not be in power if they were not the wrong sort of people.

Do you help solve problems, or are you one of them?

Automobiles continue to be driven at two speeds—lawful and awful.

How to Untangle Your Tongue

5. Double your tongue back against the rear of your mouth. Then thrust it firmly against the inside of your left cheek and then your right cheek.
6. Stick your tongue out, pointing it toward your chin and then toward your nose. Repeat rapidly several times.
7. Exaggerate tongue movements as you say these:

taw-taw-taw-taw-taw-taw-taw-taw
daw-daw-daw-daw-daw-daw-daw-daw
yaw-yaw-yaw-yaw-yaw-yaw-yaw-yaw

Behind the phony tinsel of Hollywood lies the real tinsel.

Saints are all right in heaven, but they're hell on earth. [Richard, Cardinal Cushing]

The world is a funny paper read backwards—and that way it isn't so funny.

Being unable to sleep at night is wonderful. It encourages thinking, including thinking about not thinking.

Once you're over the hill you pick up speed.

The only time a woman really succeeds in changing a man is when he's a baby. [Natalie Wood]

CLINKS AND CLANGS, HUFFS AND PUFFS, PLINKS AND PLUNKS

"Consonants can be made either by stopping the breath or by disturbing it, making it explode, or making it buzz or hum," Charlton Laird writes in his delightful *The Miracle of Language*.

Consonants make for clearness and intelligibility of our speech. Messy, slovenly articulation involves consonants far more often than vowels.

Oddly enough, your vocal cords are not involved for six of the consonants, the *voiceless* sounds. But twelve consonant sounds are *voiced* sounds, where the cords are actively involved.

How can you tell the difference? Try this:

Place your fingertips lightly against your Adam's apple. Pronounce the sounds in Column 1. (Say the sound, not the name, of the letter.) You'll feel no movement or vibration because your vocal cords aren't working. They're resting. t, p, k, s, th, f are only little molded puffs of air, *voiceless*, consonants.

But as you run through the sounds in Column 2, you'll feel some movement and vibration. For d, b, g, z, th, v, your vocal cords are working and producing extra sound to accompany the puffs of air. They're *voiced* consonants.

1	2
t (tin)	d (dock)
p (pie)	b (boy)
k (kitty)	g (girl)
s (sail)	z (zone)
th (thin)	th (that)
f (for)	v (vine)

The Crippled Consonants

There are about twenty-five consonants in the English language. Many of them aren't difficult and won't bother you. We're concerned with the eighteen troublemakers. And here they are—divided into sound families.

The Parched and Polluted Plosives

There are six plosives:

voiceless	voiced
t	d
p	b
k	g

Does the word *plosive* remind you of the word *explosive*? That's what plosives are: little explosions. Make the sound of the letter p—*not* its name—and you'll hear a popping noise. The plosives are the "drum beats" of our language.

t-d

Examples t They tell you that drugs turn you on. They don't tell you that later they turn on you.

d Judging by the divorce rate, a lot of people who said, "I do"—didn't.

How to ... Press the tip of your tongue against your upper gum ridge. The sides of your tongue should touch your side teeth. The air stream is now momentarily dammed up. Drop the tongue tip and your lower front jaw. The breath will be released in a small burst.

Faults and Foibles

8. Read this: Teddy noticed Betty standing near the bottled water.

    How did you do?

CONSERVE YOUR CONSONANTS

If you were on your toes, you hit all of those t and d sounds in the middle of the words. If you were flat-footed, you swallowed or omitted those middle plosives, and you sounded something like this mishmash: Te'y no'iced Be'y stan'-ing near the bo'led wa'er.

You're suffering from gaposis.

Do you evict medial t and d? Many of the good citizens of Baltimore, Seattle, and Houston, for example, mispronounce the names of their cities as Bal'more, Se'al, and Hous'n.

Now let's restore these sounds. Give each middle t and d a brief but solid tap as you read:

matter	after	wider	body
winter	biting	couldn't	hadn't
wouldn't	potato	candy	pardon

The atomic age is here to stay—but are we? The way to win an atomic war is to make certain it never starts.

Politics is an uncertain game. One day you're a rooster, the next you're a feather duster.

"Don't worry" is a better motto if you add the word "others."

One of the better things about getting older is that you find you're more interesting than most of the people you meet.

The cemeteries are full of people who thought the world couldn't get along without them.

9. Did you know that a Corot landscape is priddy? A twenty-five-cent piece is also called a quarder?

For contrast, do these word pairs. The words on the left need an energetic t in the middle. Be sure it's there, and be sure it's the voiceless t and not the voiced d.

matter–madder   bitter–bidder
latter–ladder   debtor–deader
batter–badder   rater–raider

There are no medial d sounds in the following material, but it's saturated with middle t sounds. Bounce them off your gum ridge. Don't substitute d.

The wheel was man's greatest invention until he got behind it.

If George Washington never told a lie, what's his picture doing on a dollar bill that's worth only forty-three cents?

Statistics are like witnesses—they will testify for either side.

Gangster "Pretty Boy" Floyd insisted that he had started out in life as an unwanted child, but by the time he was twenty-four, he was wanted in eighteen states.

Charlatan: a doctor's term for a competitor.

10. If your lips are loafing on the job, your final t and d sounds will go down the drain. You'll say jus', fac', han' and frien' instead of just, fact, hand and friend.

   Make your final plosives crystal clear and audible in these:

   Don't go to bed mad. Stay up and fight.

   Crime wouldn't pay if we let the government run it.

   Don't bite the hand that has your allowance in it.

   The only way to get rid of a temptation is to yield to it.

CONSERVE YOUR CONSONANTS

If you don't say anything, you won't be called on to repeat it.

Don't lead me; I may not follow. Don't walk behind me; I may not lead. Walk beside me and be my friend.
[Jacqueline Bisset]

11. Do you make slushy, wet t and d sounds? This will happen if you place your tongue tip on the back of your upper teeth.

Tin turns into thin; did turns into dthid.

Press the tip of your tongue against your upper gum ridge, about a third of an inch behind your teeth. You'll produce a tidy and dry t or d sound. Work for a brisk upward movement of your tongue as you read these. "Trippingly on the tongue"—advice from Shakespeare is still apropos.

teal–deal	tan–Dan	teen–dean
ten–den	Tim–dim	toll–dole
toe–doe	talk–dock	till–dill

If you drink, don't drive. Don't even putt.

Lead us not into temptation. Just tell us where it is; we'll find it.

I'm a champion. I play in the low 80s. If it's any hotter than that, I won't play. [Bob Hope]

· If you don't get everything you want, think of the things you don't get that you don't want.

I had only one friend, my dog. My wife Dottie was mad at me, and I told her a man ought to have at least two friends. Dottie agreed and bought me another dog.

HOW TO SOUND LIKE A MILLION DOLLARS

p-b

Examples p Please be careful about calling yourself an expert. An ex is a has-been, and a spurt is a drip under pressure.

b When a small boy doesn't object to soap, he's probably blowing bubbles.

How to . . . Press your lower and upper lips firmly together. As a rule, your teeth are slightly parted. The breath is compressed in your mouth. Part your lips suddenly, and the air bursts out with a light pop.

Faults and Foibles

12. "Clean up with a *damn* sponge" is the windup of a popular TV commercial in which an attractive lady is demonstrating a carpet cleaner. She obviously means *damp*, but that's not what we hear.

    Don't be a sound snipper! It's only too easy to chop off the final p or b: sleep, crab, pipe, tube.

    They're even more apt to be obliterated if they follow another consonant: chirp, bulb, trump, verb.

    If you want clean and neat p or b sounds, be sure that your lips make solid contact with each other as you shape the plosives.

    When a friend makes a mistake, don't rub it in, rub it out.

    Sound sleep is the sleep you're in when it's time to get up.

    You can't clean up this old world with soft soap. It takes grit.

    If you count sheep two at a time, you'll fall asleep twice as fast.

    "It'll soon be too hot to do the job it was too cold to do last winter," said Barb to Rip.

A compliment is the soft soap that will wipe out a dirty look.

One of the most abused words in our language? *Probably*. Most people say *prob'ly* or, worse, *pro'ly*.

Running a close second is *numer* for *number*.

Although we can understand these warped versions, they imply sloppiness. Responsible for most demolished p and b sounds are comatose lips and general lukewarm activity—and both result from carelessness and indifference.

13. Snappy, vigorous articulation is needed for the sentences below. Your lips must be locked together for p and b and then opened quickly.

The person with push will pass the person with pull.

To whip people who have iron ribs use whips of steel.

Never work before breakfast. If you have to work before breakfast, get your breakfast first.

It was not the apple on the tree, but the pair on the ground, I believe, that caused all the trouble.

No human being believes that any other human being has a right to be in bed when he himself is up.

Betty Botter bought a pound of butter. "But," she said, "this butter's bitter. If I put it in my batter, it will make my batter bitter. But a pound of better butter will make my batter better." So Betty Botter bought a pound of better butter, and it made her batter better.

k-g

Examples

k A college boy in Kentucky called his folks. He was flunking out, because it was discovered he had a clinker in his thinker.

g Doing a movie is a gamble. It's exactly like being pregnant. You're all agog, but you've got that long wait to see if it's ugly. [Carol Burnett]

How to . . . Press the back of your tongue against your soft palate (this is toward the rear of your mouth). Build up air pressure behind your tongue, and then lower your tongue abruptly, releasing the breath with a small blast.

Faults and Foibles

14. If you're asleep on the job, you'll slice and slash final k and g. Wake up and work for rugged and robust k and g sounds.

> Here Skugg lies, snug as a bug in a rug.
> If it looks like a duck, walks like a duck, and quacks like a duck—it is a duck.
> Dog catcher: a person with a seeing-dog eye.
> I have always thought of a dog lover as a dog that was in love with another dog.
> Fanatic: one with a kink, a quirk, and a crack in the cranium.
> Where all think alike, no one thinks at all.

15. What do you do about words that end in sk, sks, sked, or skt? If your articulation is a bit musty and lethargic, you do what most people do. You bypass or distort the k sounds in words such as:

CONSERVE YOUR CONSONANTS

bask   (don't say *bass*)
tasks   (don't say *tass*)
asked   (don't say *ast*)

16. The six sentences below are crammed with k and g sounds, but the kaleidoscopic spellings don't always warn you that k or g are lurking in the background. Be sure that you form k and g properly. The back of your tongue must touch your soft palate. You'll be able to feel this happen. Hear them correctly, too!

> Most people have great respect for old age—particularly if it's bottled.
>
> There are two good finishes for automobiles: lacquer and liquor.
>
> Puberty: the time when kids stop asking questions and begin to question answers.
>
> People who squawk about their income tax can be divided into two classes: men and women.
>
> A dog is a dog except when he is facing you. Then he is Mr. Dog. [Jamaican proverb]
>
> Experience is what enables you to recognize a mistake when you make it again.

17. Have a foreign language background? You may be switching g with k. You'll pronounce local as logal. Or you may be letting k go to bat for g. Pig becomes pick.

It isn't difficult to straighten them out. Don't forget that k is voiceless—a bantam breeze. There is no sound in your throat as you produce it. G is voiced. You make a minigrunt. Can you *feel* as well as *hear* the difference between the two plosives as you read this material?

HOW TO SOUND LIKE A MILLION DOLLARS

game–came	snigger–snicker	bad–back
God–cod	stagger–stacker	nag–knack
gate–Kate	lagging–lacking	sag–sack

Maggie, tack the tag on the log lock and tell Peg to put the rag on the rack.

The cad said, "I got caught playing Bach in the black bog."

Could you scold the barking dog who is digging on the cold, gold dock?

The comely kitty could not pick up the peg from the bug on the buck.

God is not a cosmic bellhop.

Plosive Smorgasbord

18. The material coming up contains all six plosives—t, d, p, b, k, g—in a variety of positions and sound combinations.

> THE TRIPLE PLAY:
>
> Do each drill line three times.
> first time:
>   Exaggerate your medial and final plosives considerably. Make them pop like a balloon. Remember, this is for practice purposes only. No one wants you to go out onto the streets exploding plosives all over the place. You might be arrested for disturbing the peace.
> second time:
>   Use moderate exaggeration. Your medial and final plosives should be medium loud pops.
> third time:
>   No exaggeration. Be natural. Tap your plosives with a feather, but tap them!

If you hit two keys on the typewriter, the one you don't want hits the paper.

Getting an award from TV is like being kissed by someone with bad breath.

What counts is not the size of the dog in the fight—it's the size of the fight in the dog.

Fewer marriages would skid if more who said, "I do," did.

A cocktail party is an excuse to drink for people who don't need any excuse.

Television isn't so bad if you don't turn it on.

If you worry about missing the boat, remember the Titanic.

Reputation is a large bubble which bursts when you try to blow it up yourself.

The company that prints those wallet cards that read: "I am a devout Catholic. In case of accident call a priest" has expanded its line to include a card which reads: "I am a devout atheist. In case of accident, good-bye."

That old bromide about truck drivers leading you to the good eats was cooked up in the same kettle as the wild tales about toads causing warts and goats eating tin cans. Don't believe it. Follow the truckers and you'll wind up at—truck stops.

If you stick a stock of liquor in your locker,
It is slick to stick a lock upon your stock,
Or some joker who is slicker's going to
trick you of your liquor,
If you fail to lock your liquor with a lock.

The Gaunt and Giddy Glides

Make the w sound in well. Hold it for a few seconds, as if you were going to say the whole word in slow motion. You'll discover that w really sounds like the oo in moon. Now move into the ell. What's your tongue doing? Moving or *gliding*, as it were. Even your lips and jaw are in motion—a smooth, continuous *gliding* action.

The problem children in the glide family are the lackadaisical l, the renegade r, and the withered w.

1

Example   Love is the feeling that you feel when you feel that you are going to feel a feeling that you never felt before.

How to ...   Place the tip of your tongue lightly against your upper gum ridge. Keep the sides of your tongue down to allow the breath stream to flow freely over the sides.

Faults and Foibles

19. Beware of mucky and shadowy l sounds!

If l is found at or near the end of a word as in ball, tale, and cold, it is a dark l. A dark l in itself certainly isn't incorrect, but if it's so dark that it's muffled and gluey, it'll probably hinder intelligibility. You'll make a too dusky l if your tongue tip doesn't contact the gum ridge.

Or do you say aw right for all right, baseba' for baseball? Then you're diluting or dumping that final l.

Don't!

As you read these, don't let those tail-end l sounds droop or lurk in the back of your throat. *Push* them forward! Give them a bit of glitter.

Striking while the iron is hot may be all right, but don't strike while the head is hot.

In real life it takes only one to make a quarrel.

There is no eel so small but that it hopes to become a whale.

We should all just smell well and enjoy ourselves a lot more.

The lion and the calf shall lie down together, but the calf won't get much sleep.

Is Melville's *Moby Dick* a tale about a real whale or a whale of a tale about a whale's tail?

20. Don't blackball *l* if it's followed by another consonant: help, silk, wolf, film.

    Do you say bid, code, jade, and wed for build, cold, jailed, and weld? If you do, you're blotching or bleaching that important l sound!

    Caution: Your tongue tip *must* make proper contact with the gum ridge as you make l in the following:

Ralph	helm	shelve	malt
self	twelve	alm	revolve
gulp	scald	film	pelvis

We are told that history always repeats itself. But, then, so does television.

A hothead seldom sets the world on fire.

There are three things most men love but never understand: females, girls, and women.

Always use first names: Remember, if God had meant us to use last names, He would have used one Himself.

A telephone pole never hits an automobile except in self-defense.

21. Here are two more boo-boos involving the l sound that you'll hear once in awhile.

    In slipshod speech, an uh sound may be wedged in between l and a preceding consonant.

                Clean changes to cuh-lean
                plenty changes to puh-lenty

If l is the final sound in a word, and if it's preceded by t or d, some speakers will blot out the plosives.

>little sounds like li-uhl or li'l
>saddle sounds like sa-uhl or sa'l

Careful listening is necessary to correct these faults. Again, check the position of your tongue, especially the tip. Try for accurate and acceptable l sounds as you say these sentences:

>When all candles are out, all cats are gray.

>All the things I really like to do are immoral, illegal, or fattening.

>Sports do not build character. They reveal it. If Howard Cosell were a sport, he would be a roller derby.

>Maybe if we could all laugh alike, and laugh at the same time, this world of ours wouldn't be able to find so many things to squabble about.

>Please pluck the plump black plums and plop them on the blue plate.

r

Example — Remember—don't call a restless man nervous; he may be wearing scratchy underwear.

How to . . . — The tip of your tongue is pointed toward the gum ridge (or curl your tongue tip back slightly toward the roof of your mouth). These are starting positions. As soon as the sound begins, your tongue glides to whatever position is necessary to make the r sound.

CONSERVE YOUR CONSONANTS

Faults and Foibles

A gremlin in our language?

The r sound is a genuine mischief-maker. It's also controversial.

Run through these five words, and you'll come up with five entirely different r sounds: rim, turn, matter, four (some Easterners pronounce it as fo-wa), fire (in some Southern speech, the r disappears completely at the ends of words—it floats off to the nearest magnolia tree—as in fah-yuh).

The section of the country in which you live may strongly influence your r sounds.

22. Wanted: a frisky tongue!

A drowsy, lifeless tongue will do much to destroy a clear and identifiable r. Let your lips be languid and listless, but your tongue needs to toil.

A little extravagance is called for here. Before you sound the r in such words as red and right, make the sound of er as in ermine and fern.

Do each of the words and sentences in this exercise twice. In the first reading, make an exaggerated er sound before the initial r:

Er-round the er-rough and er-rugged er-rock
the er-ragged er-rascal er-ran.

The second time, keep the same tongue position on the initial r which you used on the er sounds, but cut that preliminary er quite short.

rent	rim	rail	rip
rift	wren	rant	roar
raw	wrack	run	Ronald

A rose is a rose is a rose is a rose.
[Gertrude Stein]

Weathermen are never wrong. It's the weather that's wrong!

Running for money doesn't make you run fast. It makes you run first.

Real embarrassment is when you tell a girl her stockings are wrinkled and she's not wearing any.

A problem teenager is one who refuses to let his parents use the car.

23. Bugs Bunny has respectable (New Yorkish) r sounds. His nemesis, the muddled Elmer Fudd, doesn't. Elmer substitutes w: "I won't west until I get wid of that wascally wabbit."

In more elevated circles, TV newscaster Barbara Walters begets r sounds that tilt decidedly toward w. This may explain why the "Saturday Night Live" comic some years back always referred to her as "Ba-Ba-Wa-Wa."

If you find you're substituting w for r, here's how to convert to r: Keep your lips immobile, don't raise the back of your tongue, and emphasize movements of the front of your tongue as you make r.

wad–rod	way–ray	wide–ride
wade–raid	wane–rain	woo–rue
wine–Rhine	week–reek	will–rill

Rita wailed after the wild ride through the waning rain.

Are there reeds or weeds near the willows on the rill?

While waiting for the whales, Rhonda and Wanda rode the rails.

Randy Ware wooed Rhea Wheeler during the ride in the wide wagon.

The rich witch raved when the wave wrecked the rock.

CONSERVE YOUR CONSONANTS

Wheah Y'awl From?

If r is a gremlin, it's also a chameleon—a lizard that can change its color.

"You can't fool all the people all the time. Once every four years is enough."

How true! Every four years we watch and hear the two major political parties nominate candidates. There is enough hell-bubbling activity, pageantry, and speech-making for everybody. Most interesting to some of us, however, is the wonderful conglomeration of dialects or "accents."

The delegate from Boston who talks about problems that *Americker* has with *Cuber* and *Rusher* is just as colorful as the senator from South Carolina who tells the convention about his great *feah of nucleah wah*. The chairperson identifies herself as a native *Noo Yawkuh*, with an absence of recognizable r sounds, but the visiting governor of Iowa hangs onto the r in Republican as though his life depends on it (and maybe it does!). (That hard, midwestern r has been nicknamed the "Snarling R.")

Who has the correct r sound? All of them, as long as they're intelligible.

24. Back to Boston: Cuber and Rusher.

This is the *intrusive* r—an r sound where it doesn't belong. It's common in parts of New England.

If you use eastern dialect, you may be adding this extra r.

Want to eliminate it?

Practice the following sentences. Tape yourself. *Let somebody else listen to you*, and work until this tacked-on sound fades away.

Hannah Adams and Papa ought to dance the polka all day.

The gorilla understood how to eat a banana in the arena.

"The idea of doing a drama in the Alabama open-air theater is great," Anna answered.

Ole ate raw oysters in Alaska and Canada.

Georgia Upton wore the toga in the plaza in Cuba.

Eva bought the china in Vienna after the tourists went to Bulgaria.

25. Misbehaving r sounds?

Be certain they're not so quirky and nonconformist that you're hard to understand. The sound should never be lengthened or deafening.

If you have a foreign language background and trill the sound—and trilling seems to be a cross between fluttering and gargling—modify your way of making r. To get rid of the trill, use this simple procedure with your r sounds: Say uh, prolong it, and try to curl back the tip of your tongue.

Most important, if your r stands out like a beacon light, practice until you can produce a suitable r sound.

The trouble with the rat race is that even when you win, you're still a rat.

Never put off till tomorrow what you can do the day after tomorrow.

You can get away with murder in Detroit, unless you're parked next to a fire hydrant at the time.

It's real nice for children to have pets until the pets start having children.

I strongly support air bags in all new cars. I really ought to know. I married one. [Elizabeth Dole]

Vets now prescribe birth control pills for dogs. It's part of an antilitter campaign.

CONSERVE YOUR CONSONANTS

w

Example A few weeks ago we went to a well-known German restaurant. The appetizer made us queasy, and the wurst was yet to come.

How to . . . Round and push out your lips as if you were going to make the oo sound in moon (or better yet, pucker as if you were about to kiss somebody). It's the rapid activity of the lips that gives w its character. An excellent w can be produced with little or no tongue movement.

Believe it or not, you can see shoddy, slapdash articulation! W is the sound that suffers the most when your lips are allowed to hang loosely and flabbily. Amateur ventriloquists generally try to avoid material loaded with w at the beginnings of words.

Several colleagues and I once auditioned two dozen would-be radio announcers in a studio in which they were separated from us by a glass pane. We deliberately had the sound in our listening room turned off.

We quickly decided that the individuals with almost no visible lip movement had sloppy and jumbled articulation. And we also concluded that the ones with lively, active lips had supple, tangy articulation.

We gave each auditionee a second chance—with the sound turned on. Our original judgments were confirmed one hundred percent!

Faults and Foibles

26. Don't waste or wither your w sounds!
      Warning: All qu words contain w. Pronounce quack and queen as kwak and kween.
      And watch out for medial w: forward and housewife. Don't forget to pucker your lips on those sneaky w sounds.

Quickly got—quickly lost: Quite quoteworthy.

The longest word in the world is "a word from our sponsor."

A person with one watch knows what time it is. A person with two watches is never sure.

As everyone knows, there are two kinds of marriages—where the husband quotes the wife, and where the wife quotes the husband.

There is no need to worry, because the only thing to worry about is whether you are rich or poor. If you are rich, there is nothing to worry about. If you are poor, all there is to worry about is whether you are sick or well. If you are well, there is nothing to worry about. If you are sick, all you have to worry about is if you are going to get well or die. If you get well, there is no need to worry. If you die, all you have to worry about is if you go to heaven or hell. If you go to heaven, there is nothing to worry about. If you go to hell, you will be so busy shaking hands with your friends that you won't have time to worry.

27. *Sprechen Sie Deutsch?*

If German is your first language, you may confuse w with v or f. Compare the puckering position you use for w with the positions for v and f.

For v and f, your lower lip is held lightly against the edges of your upper front teeth. But for w, the lips mustn't touch your teeth.

Another little tip: As you do the words beginning with w in the material below, first say the oo of moon, hold for two seconds, and then glide into the next sound. For example: oo-ail (wail), oo-ell (well).

Check yourself in a mirror as you say these:

| vail–wail | vault–Walt | vaunt–want |
| veal–weal | vary–wary | vest–west |

CONSERVE YOUR CONSONANTS

vane–wane   veld–weld   vine–wine
vet–wet   vent–went   vee–we

Will Velma Weems give Wilbur West's vest to the vet?

Why did Violet weigh Warren Vernon and Vinnie Winson?

Van weeps when the vines and weeds are watered in winter.

Victor Wicker whispered, "We must wander with Vonnie and Wendy toward Venice."

Everybody wants to live a long time, but nobody wants to get old.

Glide Smorgasbord
28. The material coming up contains l, r, and w in a variety of positions and sound combinations.

> Try the Triple Play again as you do these.
> first time:
>   Considerable exaggeration with initial r, initial and medial w, and final l.
> second time:
>   Moderate exaggeration.
> third time:
>   No exaggeration, but make your glides bright and brawny.

The lion shall lie down with the lamb, but every morning they'll have to come up with a fresh lamb.

A quorum means enough people are there to start a quarrel.

Sign outside a Hollywood church: "Last chance to pray before entering the freeway."

Depend on the rabbit's foot if you will, but remember it didn't work for the rabbit.

The trouble with alarm clocks is that they always go off when you're asleep.

George Washington never told a lie, but then he never had to file a Form 1040.

A church bulletin: "The Lord loveth a cheerful giver. He also accepteth from a grouch."

Highway sign near Walla Walla, Washington: "Thirty days hath September, June, and November—and anyone exceeding the speed limit."

If Robin Hood were alive today, he'd steal from the poor because the rich carry only credit cards.

As the hen said when she stopped in the middle of the highway, "Let me lay it on the line."

Does beer make you strong? Yes. Try this experiment. Order a keg of your favorite brew. You'll observe that it's very heavy. Tap it and start drinking. Before too long, you'll be able to roll the keg around the room with ease.

The Neglected and Needy Nasals

Hold *a* as in calm for a few seconds, and then pinch your nostrils quite firmly. What happens? Nothing.

Now hang onto m as in hum for a few seconds, and pinch your nostrils. What happens? Everything. You can't make m if your nasal passages are stopped.

M, n, and ng are known as nasals because they are directed mostly through the nose rather than the mouth. The soft palate (velum) lowers, hanging like a curtain, and diverts the breath stream through the nasal cavities as you say the nasals in my, nine, ring.

Want to see your soft palate in action? Watch yourself in a mirror and say aw. Your soft palate will rise. Say m, and even though you can't see your soft palate perform with this sound, you'll sense that it's lowered. Say aw-m-aw-m-aw-m and you'll be able to feel the contrasting actions of the velum.

The nasal sounds not only have superb carrying power, they're not difficult to make. This explains why they're so often taken for granted.

m

Example The four most important words in the English language seem to be: I, me, mine, and money.

How to . . . Close your lips as if you were going to make the sound of b. Your tongue lies relaxed on the floor of the mouth. The air stream comes out the nose.

Faults and Foibles

29. If your speech is hurried and catch-as-catch-can, your m sounds may be corroded or they may evaporate altogether. This commonly happens if m is followed by another consonant.

    humble may sound something like hu'bl
    amnesty is contorted to anesty
    homework becomes ho'work

Most distortions can be avoided if you're certain that your lips make solid contact as you shape the m sound in this material:

I'm trying	gemlike	hymnal	aimless
simple	rammed	clamp	seemly
umbrella	company	I'm tired	lumber

When in doubt, mumble.

As the cow said to the Maine farmer, "Thank you for a warm hand on a cold morning."

Heroism: not giving a damn before witnesses.

If there is no hell, many ministers are obtaining money under false pretenses.

They call me a prima donna? Look at my face. Not a mark on it. No other champ ever looked this way. I am the champ. [Muhammad Ali]

30. Singers in pop groups and other vocal ensembles are often partial to m, as well as to the other nasals. If m occurs at the end of a word, phrase, or line, it can be stretched out into infinity. And, of course, this nasal is the sound most frequently used in humming.

Obviously in everyday talking prolonged m sounds would be ridiculously hammy. On the other hand, don't prune them. M is basically a pleasant and mellifluous sound. Give this nasal its full value and you'll enrich the sound of your speech.

The Triple Play works nicely here. Read the sentences below three times. The first time draw out m for three or four seconds. On the second reading, hold it for about two seconds. The third time, no exaggeration, but don't lop it off.

Remember—your lips must be tightly closed as you make m.

What is mind? Doesn't matter. What is matter? Never mind. [Bertrand Russell]

A camel looks like a horse that was planned by a committee.

Every person is a fool for a least five minutes every day. Wisdom consists in not exceeding the limit.

The best way to keep children home is to make the home atmosphere pleasant—and let the air out of the tires.

The chief problem about death is the fear that there may be no afterlife. Maybe I don't believe in an afterlife, but I am bringing a change of underwear.

[Woody Allen]

The only thing wrong with most monthly budgets is that there's always too much month left at the end of your money.

n

Example Never buy anything with a handle on it. It might mean work.

How to . . . Press the tip of your tongue against your gum ridge as you would for d or t. Your soft palate is lowered so that the air can exit through your nasal passages.

Faults and Foibles

31. Like its cousin m, n is repeatedly bruised and battered. When n precedes another consonant, it may be dropped altogether or transformed to an m.

    government, infantry, can meet

become

    goverment, imfantry, cameet

Remind yourself that n is a tongue-tip/upper-gum-ridge sound.

concoct	ungainly	environment	monstrous
tension	infer	gigantic	unbound
stand	tenth	unpin	lunch

Never cry over anything that can't cry over you.

I always keep a supply of gin handy in case I see a snake—which I also keep handy. [W. C. Fields]

Homicide is always a mistake. One should never do anything that one can't talk about after dinner.

One reason the Ten Commandments are so short and clear is that Moses didn't have to send them through the United Nations.

The most important part of being a salesman is confidence. Confidence is going after Moby Dick with a rowboat, a harpoon, and a jar of tartar sauce.

32. Don't be a weight-watcher!

N, in final positions, is often too thin and slim. Like m, it's a gratifying sound, and it adds ting and tingle to your speech.

Do the Triple Play again, and when you get to the third step, give n its maximum rather than its minimum value.

If your parents didn't have any children, there's a good chance you won't have any.

The dangerous age is any time between one and ninety-nine.

Accidents happen every hunting season because both hunter and gun are loaded.

The dentist's favorite marching song is "The Yanks are Coming."

Commencement speaker in Michigan: "My advice to young people who are going out into the world today—don't go!"

Tact is something that, if it is there, nobody notices it. But if it isn't there, everybody notices it.

ng

Example Acting without thinking is a lot like shooting without aiming.

How to . . . Raise the back of your tongue so that it touches the lowered soft palate. The breath stream is directed through your nose. The position of your tongue for ng is very much like that used for k and g.

Faults and Foibles

Cultured people may pronounce Tuesday as Tooz-day instead of Tyooz-day. Who'll criticize? Nobody.

Educated people may say when as wen instead of hwen. No one will get excited about it.

But those who persist in saying comin', goin', thinkin', sleepin' may be askin' for trouble.

This mannerism is known as "dropping the g"—a totally inaccurate description, by the way, because there is rarely a hard g (as in gag) in most ng sounds. It's a speech idiosyncrasy found all over the country, not, as many believe, only in the South.

A beloved old speech professor of mine said many years ago, "There are four kinds of cheating that will catch up with you sooner or later: at poker, on your income tax return, on your spouse, and on your final ng sounds."

Probably most people who cheat on this sound know better, too. So why do they say, "Be seein' you"? It has something to do with the "Let's-be-one-of-the-crowd" or "I-don't-want-to-be-different-from-the-others" syndrome.

Oddly enough, soap opera actors and actresses are primary offenders. And believe it or not, there are highly talented performers among them, and *they*, of all people, really ought to know better!

Recently Mark, a bright young college graduate of a large midwestern university, interviewed for an exciting and well-paying position with a major insurance company. He was a Phi Beta Kappa with excellent references, charm, zest, and princely good looks. But Mark was never known to have pronounced a final ng in his life. He lost out to a young man with a C+ average who had excellent speech habits.

The executive personnel director explained the decision to Mark's dean: "Mark is an otherwise well-qualified young man, but he mauls his speech. He's an ng-dropper. We're fussy about this sort of thing. We insist on hiring people who are verbally fastidious."

33. Say slowly n (as in sin) and ng (as in sing):

> n-ng-n-ng-n-ng-n-ng

Notice the basic difference in tongue position between the two sounds?

The n is formed with the front part, the tip, or point, of your tongue.

Ng is shaped with the back of your tongue.

Remember this distinction as you practice these:

kin–king	lawn–long	gun–gung	tan–tang
run–rung	hun–hung	gone–gong	ton–tongue
sun–sung	thin–thing	pin–ping	win–wing

34. Read this nonsense material slowly. (Note: Read *across* the columns, from left to right.) Concentrate on the difference between the articulation of n and ng.

> Get the feel of n as a tip-of-the-tongue sound and of ng as a back-of-the-tongue sound.

fan	fang	fan-in	fang-in	fang-ing
sin	sing	sin-in	sing-in	sing-ing
ban	bang	ban-in	bang-in	bang-ing

35. The person who says wearin' for wearing would have no problem at all if asked to pronounce only the last four letters of the word. He would certainly say ring rather than rin.

    Over-articulate as you practice these. The words are divided in a purely mechanical fashion. Whenever you see a double diagonal line, pause for a second or two, eliminating any kind of vocal sound.

    ring/ /ring/ /ring: ar/ /ring,   soar/ /ring, hear/ /ring,
                        bar/ /ring, sour/ /ring, pour/ /ring,
                        mar/ /ring, stir/ /ring, star/ /ring

    Now, eliminating the pause, connect the two syllables and say them rapidly. Can you make a firm ng at the end of each word?

36. Be grateful! Ng is found only in central or final positions. As you work with this material, be supercautious. Don't let n weasel its way in and take over for ng.

    Having read so much about the bad effects of smoking, they decided to give up reading.

    The cost of living is going up, and the chance of living is going down.

    Some folks get what's coming to them by waiting; others, while crossing the street.

    Shunning women, liquor, gambling, smoking, and eating will not make one live longer. It will only seem like it.

    Unhappiness is being trapped on a rainy highway with a slow-moving truck in front of you and a fast-moving truck coming up behind you.

A digital clock is something they have in an office so you can tell how long you must wait before you can start stopping work by stalling until.

37. Are you from the East—particularly the New York Brooklyn-Bronx areas? If you are, you may want to scrutinize this section. If you aren't, move on to Exercise 41.

Say: singer, linger.

Both words have an ng. Did you notice, however, that the ng is not pronounced the same way?

In singer, the ng is simply the nasal sound we've been working on. There is no plosive hard g (as in gag) in the word. You say sing-er.

In linger, the ng is a combination of the nasal ng *plus* the plosive (hard) g. You say ling-ger.

No wonder, then, that we sporadically have trouble with ng. Fiendish English spelling doesn't help either. To add to the turmoil, in certain foreign languages and dialects, ng is almost invariably followed by a g or k. Individuals whose language backgrounds include Yiddish, Slavic, Spanish, Hungarian, or Italian—even though they may be native-born—often add the villainous "Long Guyland click." Gong becomes gong-g or gong-k, ring becomes ring-g or ring-k.

How can the hard g be purged?

Your sense of hearing and feeling will help. You'll remember that the back of your tongue is raised against the velum or soft palate to make ng. Say sing and you'll *feel* the contact.

Say sing again, but this time listen quite conscientiously to the nasal sound, extend it a few seconds, and as you're holding ng, pull your tongue away from the velum. If this is done, you won't add the hard g.

Read this material slowly, always drawing out ng. Pull your tongue away from your velum *during* the production

CONSERVE YOUR CONSONANTS

of the nasal rather than *after*, and you'll probably exterminate the after-click.

thing	sing	ring	spring
bang	long	bong	going
wrong	rang	clang	hang

38. Fasten your seatbelts!

    Now that we've told you how to remove the after-click, let's put it back in! You *do not* use it with such words as long, young, and strong. But you *do* use it with the comparative and superlative forms:

    longer (long-ger) longest (long-gest)

    stronger (strong-ger) strongest (strong-gest)

    If you find ng within the root or the middle of a word, it's generally pronounced with the click: ng-g.

finger	extinguish	kangaroo	English
fungus	anger	mingle	tingle
hunger	single	angry	bungle

And to spoil the fun—the exceptions: gingham, Washington, hangar, strength, length.

Even outstanding speakers slip on these pesky and temperamental sounds. When in doubt, consult your dictionary.

Nasal Smorgasbord

Don't neglect your nasals! Nourish them!

39. A reminder—

    m: your lips must be firmly closed;
    n: the tip of your tongue must be placed against your upper gum ridge;
    ng: the rear of your tongue must make contact with your velum.

The Triple Play works beautifully with these sounds. And at the third level—even without the overplaying—make m, n, and ng glisten. Above all, be accurate.

Dentistry means drilling, filling, and billing.

If you know beans about chili, you know chili has no beans.

There are still a few people who believe in getting up and getting, while a great many people prefer sitting down and sitting.

An alcoholic is not one who drinks too much, but one who can't drink enough.

The sighing tinker from Bingham hung the shingle on the hangar.

Never murder a man who is committing suicide.

What this country needs is a good five-second TV commercial.

Basically my wife is immature. I'd be home in the bath and she'd come in and sink my boats. [Woody Allen]

Women generally manage to love the guy they marry more than they manage to marry the guy they love.

My advice to you: Don't ask, "Who am I, what am I doing here, where am I going?" Just enjoy your ice cream while it's on your plate—that's my philosophy. [Tennessee Williams]

There's music all around you if you just listen. There's as much music in belching as in Beethoven, munching meatballs as in Mozart, in the sound of a toilet flushing as there is in Tartini. [John Cage]

The Fizzy and Fractured Fricatives

Fricative = Friction. Right? Right!
Say sizzle. You'll notice you're putting obstructions in

CONSERVE YOUR CONSONANTS

your mouth that interrupt the outgoing breath stream. The air is forced through a small, narrow opening or slit. A noise is produced by friction, and it sounds that way.

The fricatives are the buzzers and the blasters of the consonant tribe. The six major offenders are s, z, th (thin), t̶h̶ (there), f, and v.

STOP HERE!

Forget the Triple Play!

The extreme/moderate/no exaggeration pattern works wonderfully with plosives, glides, and nasals. It does NOT work with fricatives.

As you get into this material, don't overdo. Don't puff up your fricatives. *Underdo.*

S-Z

Examples s Sign in a bakery window in San Francisco: "Cakes—sixty-six cents. Upside-down cakes—ninety-nine cents."

z Rock music is amazing. It includes a zestful vocalist who sings off key and a noisy drummer who doesn't like music.

How to . . . Raise the sides of your tongue so that they touch the middle and back upper teeth. A thin stream of air is forced through a V-shaped groove along the midline of your tongue. Your tongue tip is in a similar position for t. (CAUTION: S and z are kissing cousins. Anything said about the voiceless s also applies to the voiced z.)

Faults and Foibles

Gas guzzlers? Big cars—according to people who dislike them.

Breath guzzlers? S and z. They're one-sound cyclones.

Listen to a group of people recite material in unison—responsive readings by a congregation are a fine example—and you'll hear waves of hisses that belong in a snake pit.

A majority of the hissers are probably articulating the sound correctly. What they're doing incorrectly is simply producing too much of it. Even a respectable, normal s is rackety and turbulent. If you're making an s that sounds like a tornado, reduce your breath pressure. Don't emphasize the sound! Don't strong-arm it! Don't hang onto it. S should be cut short, touched lightly and briefly—but not allowed to vanish entirely.

40. For contrast and to help you hear the difference between a good, skimpy s and a long, fat s, read these word pairs aloud. Build up the s in the first word of each pair as the spelling indicates. Make it sound like a minor monsoon.

    In the second word of the pair, tap the sound as if touching a hot stove, and hurry on to the following vowel sounds. Stress the vowels instead.

    s-s-s-s-see–see   s-s-s-s-sad–sad
    s-s-s-s-so–so   s-s-s-s-saw–saw
    s-s-s-s-say–say   S-S-S-S-Sue–Sue

Work for an unobtrusive s and z. Don't blow them to smithereens. Condense and compress. Make them quiet.

zigzag	lesson	gossip	lizard
Sam	sort	sod	Zulu
hiss	craze	has	lazy

There's an old southern saying: If it ain't busted, why fix it?

It's what the guests say as they swing out of the driveway that counts.

She's somewhere between the age of consent and collapse.

You must learn from the mistakes of others. You can't possibly live long enough to make them all yourself.

Scratch the surface, and if you're lucky, you'll find more surface.

41. "Whistler's s" is even more galling than the overdone, gusty s described in Exercise 40. The speech of individuals with gaps between their front teeth or people with poorly fitting dentures is often afflicted with "Whistler's s."

    It's an irksome and high-pitched sound. To anyone who works with a microphone, it's a serious handicap. Electronic amplification can turn a minor whistle into a howling wind.

    Is your tongue too tense? Or are you pressing the tip of your tongue tightly against your upper teeth? You'll produce a thin or sharp squeak. Relaxing your tongue a bit may get rid of it. "Whistler's s" also occurs if you let your lower lip touch your upper front teeth while making the sound. Bear in mind that clean s sounds require that the lips be curled away from the teeth sufficiently to keep the edges of the teeth free.

    Before you read the material in this exercise, hiss s, holding your tongue in slightly different positions. Then draw the tip back. Listen carefully as you experiment until you can find a satisfactory position.

moss	hits	loose	psalm
sass	mats	mace	sissy
loss	ropes	deuce	juice

The world is a rose. Smell it and pass it to your friends.

The devil does a nice business, considering he has such a lousy location.

About peace, when all is said and done, more is said than done.

The very moment everything looks serene, all hell breaks loose.

In politics, if you want anything said, ask a man. If you want anything done, ask a woman.
[Margaret Thatcher]

42. Let's put it all together.

If you've been smearing s (thay for say) or liquifying it (shlay for say), a final check will help you banish these frazzled fricatives.

Take note: They're *not* plosives. Don't blast them out. Fricatives should be pint-sized and knife-edged. But don't disregard them.

And finally, is your tongue position correct? That t position will help you with most s sounds.

The first screw to get loose in your head is the one that holds your tongue in place.

Gossip is when you hear something you like about someone you don't.

In times like these, it always helps to recall that there have always been times like these.

It is with narrow-souled people as with narrow-necked bottles, the less they have in them the more noise they make in pouring out.

The fool says, "Don't put all your eggs in one basket." But the wise person says, "Put all your eggs in one basket and—*watch that basket!*"

(rapidly as possible)
Swan swim over the sea;
Swim, swan, swim.
Swan swim back again;
Well swum, swan.

CONSERVE YOUR CONSONANTS

th-th̸

Examples

th Let's be thankful we're living in a country where we can say what we think without thinking.

th̸ There ought to be a less loathesome way of starting the day than having to get up.

How to . . . Thrust your flattened tongue tip between your teeth so that the upper side makes a soft contact with the lower edge of the upper teeth. Drive the breath between your tongue and teeth. (Anything said about th also applies to th̸.)

Faults and Foibles

What's the hardest-to-pronounce short word in the English language? SIXTHS.

It's a fine example of a one-word tongue twister. The chances are that you don't pronounce it correctly. If you say it this way: s-i-k-s

you're wrong.

Now say it in slow motion: s-i-k-s-th-s

and you're right.

(But try it rapidly and see what happens!)

Th happens to be a persnickety sound, and it's a tough one to pronounce in sixths. It can be almost as formidable in simple words.

If you've ever seen old-time gangster movies from the 30s—James Cagney and Edward G. Robinson starred in a few dozen—you'll recall that many of the characters couldn't say these, them, or mother. They used a Brooklyn-Mafia/Chicago-mobster dialect that turned th into d: dese, dem, mudder.

One doesn't necessarily have to be a thug to mess up th sounds. The d substitute is heard not infrequently among those who use Eastern dialect. (Remember a Bronx-born Hollywood star who achieved immortality for his delivery of this line: "Yonduh lies duh castle of my fadduh"?)

HOW TO SOUND LIKE A MILLION DOLLARS

Some easterners permit the tongue to make too firm a contact against the edges of the teeth. A sound something like t or d will result. Remind yourself that t and d require a close tongue-tip contact, but that the contact for th must be light as fluff.

43. If you're substituting t or d for th, try this:

Extend your tongue so that the broad part of it touches your upper front teeth. Force out air as you gradually retract your tongue until the tip reaches the upper teeth. When you can make a healthy sound, try the material in this exercise. Be certain that the contact is gentle for good th sounds, but solid for t and d.

thin–tin	oath–oat	death–debt
thought–taught	thank–tank	three–tree
thigh–tie	theme–team	author–otter

Miss Diss said this: "Thanks for putting the tanks near the three trees."

The truth hurts—especially on the bathroom scales.

The thicker one gets with some people, the thinner they become.

The Lord giveth and the IRS taketh away.

Theophilus Thistle, the thistle-sifter, sifted a sieve of unsifted thistles. If Theophilus Thistle, the thistle-sifter, sifted a sieve of unsifted thistles, where is the sieve of unsifted thistles Theophilus Thistle, the thistle-sifter, sifted?

44. What's the difference between the th sounds in Column 1 and Column 2?

1	2
thin	thou
bath	bathe
ether	either

Your tongue position is exactly the same for both.

The th sounds in Column 1 are voiceless puffs of air. Your vocal cords are not vibrating.

The th sounds in Column 2 are voiced. Your vocal cords are vibrating and producing extra little rumbles to go along with the puffs.

Spelling never tells you which is which. Your ear does, however. It's no problem hearing the difference between the two sounds.

There seems to be a trend toward using the voiceless th (thin) at the expense of its voiced cousin—th (the). Avoid mistaking one for the other as you do these:

When you get there—North Dakota—there isn't any there there.

The person who thinketh by the inch and speaketh by the yard should be kicketh by the foot.

Writers seldom write the things they think. They simply write the things they think other people think they think.

What, oh what, is thought? It is the only thing—and yet nothing.

There's no such thing as a tough child. If you parboil them first for three or four hours, they always come out tender. [W. C. Fields]

If you burn the candle at both ends you are not as bright as you think.

45. The most common word in the English language? I. The second most common? The.

Few of us have problems with the pronoun. Quite a few of us of us get addled with the article.

If you say: "THEE higher you get in THUH evening, THEE lower you feel in THEE morning"—your THEE and THUH are reversed.

The rules are simple.

The is pronounced THUH if it's followed by a consonant: THUH girl, THUH book, THUH zebra.

The is pronounced THEE if it's followed by a vowel: THEE apple, THEE Indian, THEE onion.

If you're keen-eyed as you read, you won't confound THEE with THUH.

The emptier the pot, the quicker the boil—watch your temper.

The expressway is a highway with three lanes—the right lane, the left lane, and the one you're in when you see the exit.

It's not the ups and downs of life that bother the average man. It's the jerks.

It is often the last key on the ring that opens the door.

You can't deal with the serious things in the world unless you understand the amusing things first.

46. "Zee trouble wis zee French is zat zay seem wiser zan zay are," the late Charles DeGaulle once said.

Very few foreign languages have our th sound. If your first language is French or German, for example, you may be saying zeez and sink for these and think.

If you're substituting s or z for th, you're doing something wrong with the tip of your tongue.

For s or z: Raise your tongue tip toward, but not in actual contact with, the upper gum ridge.

For th: Place your tongue tip lightly against the back or the edges of your upper front teeth.

Check your tongue position carefully as you read this material. No s or z substitutions for th.

thought–sought	breathe–breeze
thigh–sigh	thumb–sum
south–souse	rather–razzer

Truth crushed to earth will rise again—but so will a lie.

If health is wealth, how come it's tax-free?

They threw three thick things at the thirty-three thin thugs.

The young never understand youth in others; that is their tragedy. The old always do; that is theirs.

Few people think more than three times a year. I have made a great reputation for myself by thinking three times a week. [Germaine Greer]

f-v

Examples f Don't sweat the small stuff. It's all stuff. If you can't flow, flee.

v Drive toward others as you would have others drive toward you.

How to . . . Raise your lower lip, drawing it inward, and place it lightly against the edges of your upper front teeth. Then force the breath stream between the lip and teeth.

Faults and Foibles

F and v have something in common with s: A little bit of them goes a long way.

Too much hissing air on these sounds will make you sound like those two felines, Garfield and Morris, spatting at the top of a fence. Save your breath and work for razor-edged f or v sounds.

47. Bear in mind that a spic-and-span f or v depends mostly on the activity of the lower lip. If your lip is protruded or drawn back too far, you'll be producing fleshy and fuzzy fricatives. That lower lip must make an easy contact with your upper front teeth as you come out with the sounds.

> Even the lion has to defend itself against flies.
>
> Figures won't lie, but liars will figure.
>
> When our vices have left us, we flatter ourselves that we have left them.
>
> You might as well fall flat on your face as lean too far backwards.
>
> Wagner's music has some wonderful moments, but awful half-hours.
>
> It isn't the cough that carries you off; it's the coffin they carry you off in.

Frowzy articulation? Here's an example:
A lotta people sorta have a lotta free time.

> A lot of people also love to carve up that poor, impotent little word, of. True, it's runty and inconspicuous, but that doesn't justify squashing it. Of, although spelled with an f, is pronounced with a v.

48. Go over this material slowly a few times, and then gradually increase your speed to a normal rate. Be conscious of the lip-to-teeth articulation as you make a v at the end of each of.

full of people	bunch of girls
bag of peanuts	tired of him
lots of money	rows of seats

> For those who like this sort of thing, this is the sort of thing they like.

There are Ten Commandments, right? Well, it's kind of like an exam. You get eight out of ten right, you're just about top of the class.

Beware of the high cost of low living.

Lots of us think our national anthem should be changed to "Deep in the Heart of Taxes."

I am a member of the human race. That means a little of the angel and a little of the devil.

Anyone who learns English as a second language (especially if the first is German or Spanish) tends to pronounce v as f or b.

49. "Fince can proof that foodoo is a file fice" (German speakers)

or

"Bince can probe that boodoo is a bile bice" (Spanish speakers).

It is, of course, "Vince can prove that voodoo is a vile vice."

(German speakers may also mix up v and w. See Exercise 27 in this chapter.)

For f-v confusion: You'll be able to *feel* as well as *hear* the difference. F is a voiceless air puff—no vibration in your throat as you make the sound. V is voiced—there'll be a minicommotion in your Adam's apple.

feel–veal	rifle–rival
fan–van	strife–strive
define–divine	half–have

For b-v confusion: b is a plosive, of course, and to make it you must press your lips closely together. To sound v, you should feel your lower lip touching your upper teeth.

ban–van	best–vest
dub–dove	saber–saver
base–vase	lubber–lover

118
HOW TO SOUND LIKE A MILLION DOLLARS

Don't get befuddled with the voiceless f and the voiced v in the sentences below. And remind yourself that b is a lips-firmly-together sound, but v is a lower-lip-against-upper-teeth sound.

You haven't lived until you've died in California.

Reckless drivers drive like living is going out of style.

Shakespeare said that the evil men do lives after them. On TV this is called a rerun.

Have you noticed that people who have stopped smoking haven't stopped talking about it?

The male lovebug on the average devotes fifty-six hours of its life to making love. The lifespan of the lovebug is fifty-seven hours.

Fricative Smorgasbord

50. The material below contains s, z, th, th, f, and v in a variety of positions and sound combinations.

Nip, snip, and clip these windy sounds. Be stingy!

If only God would give me a clear sign. Like making a large deposit in my name in a Swiss bank.
[Woody Allen]

Roses are red, violets are blue. I'm a schizophrenic, and so am I.

My dog thinks I'm his best friend. Which is pretty amazing, considering I'm the one who had him fixed.
[David Letterman]

Never exaggerate your faults. Leave that for your friends.

"I mourn death, I disperse the lightning, I announce the Sabbath, I rouse the lazy, I scatter the winds, I appease the bloodthirsty." [Inscription on an old bell]

The skunk sat on a stump. The skunk thunk the stump stunk, but the stump thunk the skunk stunk.

More homes are destroyed by fusses than by funerals or fires.

The secret of success is to start from scratch and keep on scratching.

Sex appeal is fifty percent what you've got and fifty percent what people think you've got. [Sophia Loren]

It doesn't take brains to criticize; any old vulture can find a carcass.

A good question to ask ourselves: What kind of a world would this world be if everybody was just like me?

Grab Bag: Review Material for All the Crippled Consonants

Wanted: lips that are lithe, limber, and lissome.

51. This material highlights sounds that are produced by the action of your lips. Your lips are more than just two fleshy flaps forming the margin of your mouth. For adept, precise articulation, make their movements spry and perky.

p b m w

When you're about to meet your maker it makes you meeker.

One of the quickest ways to learn how to think on your feet is to become a pedestrian.

The world is full of willing people—some willing to work, the rest willing to let them.

Politician's prayer: Yea, even though I graze in pastures with jackasses, I pray that I will not bray like one.

A bank is a place where they lend you an umbrella in fair weather and ask for it back again when it begins to rain.

There was a pious man who went to bed thinking he had God Almighty by the little finger, but woke up to find that he had the devil by the big toe.

Don't inflate those fricatives!

52. This material features sounds made by placing the lower lip against the upper teeth. These two sounds have a tendency to become bulky and buzzy. They should always be slender and subdued.

f v

Fog: stuff that is dangerous to drive in—especially if it's mental.

Fancy free: a fancy way to say "playing the field."

Football: a game where the spectators have four quarters in which to kill a fifth.

One of the strangest things about life is that the poor who need money the most are the very ones who never have it.

TV: where you can see the movies you've been avoiding for years.

Have you fifty friends? It is not enough. Have you one enemy? It is too much!

It's O.K. to stick your tongue out!

53. This material underscores sounds that are formed by placing the tip of the tongue between or against the front teeth. If you're substituting s or z for th (zem instead of them),

you're desecrating the sound. If you substitute t or d for th (brudder instead of brother), you're violating it. Be meticulous about tongue placement. Don't overpower these sounds.

th th̸

There are mighty few people who think what they think they think.

Thief: one who has the habit of finding things just before people miss them.

The afternoon: that part of the day we spend thinking about how we wasted the morning.

Sending an offspring through college is very educational. It teaches both the mother and the father how to do without a lot of things.

There are two kinds of directors in the theater: those who think they are God and those who are certain of it.

The marvelous thing about a joke with a double meaning is that it can only mean one thing.

Let your tongue hop, skip and jump!

54. This material accentuates sounds that are shaped by placing the tip or blade of the tongue on or near the upper gum ridge. A deft and dexterous tongue will help. (And don't turn s into a hurricane, please!)

t d l s z n

There are three kinds of lies: lies, damned lies, and statistics.

The length of a minute depends on which side of the bathroom door you're on.

Since God made Adam out of dust He had to make Eve to settle him.

I get my exercise acting as pallbearer to my friends who exercise.

Always keep your head up, but be careful to keep your nose on a friendly level.

Try as much as possible to be wholly alive, with all your might, and when you laugh, laugh like hell and when you get angry, get good and angry. Try to be alive. You'll be dead soon enough. [Joan Rivers]

Your tongue: Inert? No! Alert? Yes!

55. This material showcases a sound that is created by raising the tongue toward the front of the hard palate. A limp and langorous tongue will hurt your r sound. Your lips can be dormant for r, but energize your tongue!

r

Pleasure is more trouble than trouble.

A wrong reason is worse than no reason at all.

Hard work never hurts people who don't do any.

There is only one religion, though there are a hundred different versions of it.

Nothing beats a cold shower before breakfast except no cold shower before breakfast.

Drive carefully! Remember: It's not only a car that can be recalled by its maker.

Meek and mild? No! Grab for the gusto!

56. This material emphasizes sounds that are molded by pressing the back of the tongue against the soft palate or velum

(toward the rear of the mouth). Make muscular sounds of k and g, and don't let ng do a disappearing act. Ng is *not* n!

k g ng

 In the kingdom of the deaf, the person with one ear is king.

 If I can't brag of knowing something, then I brag of not knowing it. At any rate—brag!

 One way to prevent conversation from being boring is to say the wrong thing.

 The Lord gave us two ends—one for sitting and the other for thinking.

 Colleges teach the dead languages as if they were buried and the living ones as if they were dead.

 The brain is a wonderful organ. It starts working the moment you get up in the morning, and doesn't stop until you get to the office.

5
Varnish Your Vowels

Say ah-h-h as you do when the doctor checks your throat. You've made a vowel sound, and you noticed that there was virtually no obstruction of the breath stream as you formed the ah.

Now make these sounds: p and z. You have to set up an obstacle course inside of your mouth to block the air stream in order to produce consonants.

> *Vowels are made with a more or less open mouth and without blocking the air stream. Vowels are free from friction noises.*

Consonants provide beginnings, middles, and endings of words. As Alexander Graham Bell said it, "Consonants constitute the backbone of spoken language—vowels, the flesh and blood."

As you did with *"The Haunted House,"* tape *"Knock Thrice Before You Enter."* The vowels and diphthongs in bold type are capable of all kinds of shenanigans. At the end of the story is a checklist that will help you determine where specific improvement is needed.

KNOCK THRICE BEFORE YOU ENTER

[**A**]   Back in the days of castles and dragons, there lived a Count **A**delbert and his n**a**gging wife, **A**gnes. It was **a**n unhappy marriage.

VARNISH YOUR VOWELS

She demanded that Adelbert pamper her. One afternoon Agnes was found dead in her bath. Strange marks on her neck hinted that the damsel might have been strangled, but no one dared ask Adelbert about the marks.

[B] In a big villa down the road lived the recently widowed Princess Isabella. She was nineteen, pretty, and spirited. Adelbert proposed. The Princess shilly-shallied for a few weeks and then agreed to marry him. Tedium quickly set in. Adelbert was fifty-five and a weak and indifferent lover, and he spent a great deal of his time sleeping. Isabella became impatient and bored. Into this grievous scene one day rode the handsome and appealing young Philip, an itinerant minstrel with a magnificent singing voice.

[C] Adelbert welcomed the pleasant, gentle fellow. That night, after an elegant and festive meal, Philip was asked to sing. Adelbert fell asleep in front of all the guests. Philip's melodies became more and more intense and ecstatic and, of course, they were directed at Isabella. Philip felt in his bones that the enchanting lady wanted him. How could he get to her? God helps them who help themselves, thought the zealous Philip.

[D] He found out that the Count and Countess had separate but adjoining bedrooms. The Count visited his wife twice a week. He would pound on her door three times, and announce: "I, the Count, am here to bring joy to the Countess." Then he entered.

Two nights later Philip knocked on Isabella's door three times and also entered. Philip had an enjoyable hour or two. Isabella thought he was the Count.

About fifteen minutes after Philip left, the real Count was at the door. Said the astounded Isabella, "Within this very hour you left my couch. At your age, shouldn't you be more careful?"

The Count frowned and went immediately to the sleeping wing of the castle.

Adelbert reasoned that whoever had just spent an hour with his wife would still be in a highly excited state. His heart would be pounding. Philip realized why the Count was there. Although the frightened singer was not a coward, his own heart started thumping noisily. Out of his half-closed eyes, he watched the outraged Count go to each sleeper and feel his heart.

Finally he came to Philip. "Aha!" said the scowling Count. "Here is the foul, vile culprit. It's too dark for me to see who it is, but I have a fine idea."

The jealous spouse produced a pair of scissors and cut off most of the hair on the right side of Philip's head and then departed. Philip panicked. "Alas, I am destroyed. They will boil me in oil."

Then he had a bright idea. He found the scissors which Adelbert had left behind and went from bed to bed cutting off huge gobs of hair from the right side of each sleeper's head.

The next day growling Adelbert ordered the entire household to appear in front of him. Fifty men lined up—every one of them trimmed on the right side. The annoyed Count sighed. "One of you is a scoundrel, but he's no fool. Let him who did it dare not do it again. Now, go in peace, all of you!"

[Freely adapted from Boccaccio]

Checklist for *Knock Thrice Before You Enter*

In Section A— the sound in bold type is a vowel: a (as in at)

Did you...

Transform and into end, fat into fit? Strain on *a*, making a metallic, clangy sound? Push *a* through your nose so that it sounded like a nasal siren?

In Section B— the sounds in bold type are vowels: i (as in it) ee (as in be)

Did you...

Sneak in an extra little grunt and turn big into bi-uhg, live into li-uhv? Juggle these sounds and say heem for him, gravus for grievous?

In Section C— the sound in bold type is a vowel: e (as in red)

Did you...

Barter e? Trade deadly for daidly, fell for fill?

Detour through your nose? Allow e, in a word like melt, to slip through your nasal cavities?

You're beating up your vowels! You're also attaching barnacles to them. Look in on the vowels in this chapter.

In Section D— the sounds in bold type are diphthongs (a diphthong is a blend of two vowels): ou (as in house), oi (as in oil), i (as in my)

Did you...

Scream and screech on ou, producing an edgy, high-strung sound like a cat with a migraine?
Convert right to rahuht or raht?
Swerve and let ow veer through your nose?
Twist oi into er and say verse instead of voice?
Soften oi and turn adjoin into adjine?

You're dissipating and downgrading your diphthongs. Upgrade them! Do your daily dozen with the material on diphthongs in Chapter 6.

THE VIOLATED VOWELS

There are about fifteen vowel sounds in our language. Eleven of them are easily manageable. Four of them are unruly. The rambunctious ones are:

    a as in ask   i as in fit
    ee as in feet   e as in bet

a

Example   The family you come from isn't half as important as the family you're going to have.

How to . . .   Let your tongue lie almost flat on the floor of your mouth, but keep it well forward. Your tongue muscles should be quite lax.

Faults and Foibles

1. Cats are cute in Broadway musicals and on Hallowe'en, but not so captivating if they take up residence in your throat.

    The most common problem with a is making it with

a nervous, nasal, and meowlike quality. This is particularly noticeable in eastern speech. Not a few citizens of the New York, Philadelphia, and Baltimore areas, for example, are apt to fashion a very taut and unpleasant sound.

(In the sample sentence you're about to read, eh is the e sound of egg, men.)

The cat people say, "Eh-usk the meh-un bout the teh-un heh-ut." (Ask the man about the tan hat.)

This type of bleak, dry, and disagreeable distortion often results from an overtense tongue that is raised too high. A closed and locked jaw also adds to the screechy-scratchy, cat-on-a-hot-tin-roof quality.

Speakers in other sections of the country must also be careful with this sound. If *a* is near a nasal sound (m, n, ng) or a plosive (t, d, p, b, k, g), it can easily slip into a tinny, jangling mutilation.

Try this experiment with the word pairs below. *The negative*: On the first word of each pair, *deliberately* tense your tongue, tighten and close your jaw somewhat, and be as nasal as you can. As you pounce on each of the eh sounds, think of saying the word egg between clenched teeth. *The positive*: On the second member of each pair, work for a tranquil, almost-lazy tongue. Open your jaw, and be on guard against nasality.

beh-un–ban   deh-un–Dan
reh-un–ran   teh-ung–tang
feh-un–fan   heh-ud–had

Can you carry over the more restful and pleasant *a* of the second word in the above pairs as you say these? (And say them rapidly.)

ban-shan-han-van-can-lamb-tram
jam-jab-sap-tab-Ann-sack-hack
ma'am-map-mack-mass-mab-man-mat

VARNISH YOUR VOWELS

Don't wring *a* out of shape. Avoid undue tongue and jaw tensions or nasality as you read these sentences. Stay with them until you can make an uncatlike a.

> Every man has it in his power to make one woman happy by remaining a bachelor.
>
> He who laughs last didn't get the joke.
>
> Marriage is like canned hash. You've got to take a chance.
>
> As for bad taste, it is, in fact, like bad breath— better than no breath at all.
>
> Tax the farmer, tax his fowl;
> Tax his dog, tax his howl.
> Tax his horse and tax his bed;
> Tax the bald spot on his head.
> Tax his ox, tax his ass;
> Tax his auto, tax his gas.
> Tax the coffins, tax the shrouds;
> Tax the souls beyond the clouds.
> Tax them all and tax them well,
> And do your best to make life hell.
>
> [Anonymous]

2. "If I Had My Druthers," a popular tune of the 1950s, suggested that Appalachian mountain folk pronounce *rather* as *ruther*. This is possibly true, but folksy mispronunciation is also encountered in other sections of the country.

The paired words below do *not* rhyme.

> Reminder: For a: Your tongue is almost flat on the floor of your mouth.
>
> For u: Raise the center of your tongue slightly.

dam–dumb   clack–cluck
fan–fun   tan–ton
bad–bud   ram–rum

Some people turn had into head and can into kin.
For e: The back of your tongue touches your upper molars.

bat–bet	sand–send
dack–deck	fan–fen
chat–chet	ham–hem

For i: The front of your tongue is relatively high.

sack–sick	mat–mit
had–hid	dapper–dipper
salve–sieve	ham–him

Monitor yourself diligently as you read these sentences. Don't let u, e, or i slink in and replace a.

Tex Thaxter, the actor, pays taxes on taxis in Texas.

Sam Goldwyn once said: "This makes me so mad it gets my dandruff up."

People with tact have less to retract.

Mick Jagger had a bad accident recently. One of his pals slammed the car door on his hair.

Never gamble in heavy traffic. The cars may be stacked against you.

ee

Example Some preachers and teachers don't talk in their sleep; they talk in other people's sleep.

How to ... Arch the front of your tongue high and far forward so that it almost touches your hard palate (the roof of your mouth). The tongue should be tense. Your lips are spread slightly, and your upper and lower teeth are quite close together.

Faults and Foibles
"Did Mr. Kee-uhl stee-uhl your whee-uhls?"
Some southerners and quite a few users of General American dialect—particularly those in midwestern regions—occasionally insert an extra little sound—an uh—after the ee, especially if it's followed by an l.

This uh sound is one hundred percent legitimate in words such as: about (uh-bout), lion (li-uhn), sofa (sof-uh).

But if you stick it in where it doesn't belong, it's *illegitimate*. Incidentally, many educated people add this extra uh in certain words: we'll kneel becomes we-uhl knee-uhl. This generally doesn't interfere with understanding. So—to uh or not to uh? It's up to you.

3. Want to stamp out illegitimacy?
Read the word pairs below. You'll have no difficulty pronouncing the e in the first word of each pair. Then transfer the same e to the second word without inserting uh. *Hold your jaw steady on each second word.* If your jaw drops, this means you're stuffing in an uh where it shouldn't be.

keen–keel	read–reel
peek–peel	seen–seal
mean–meal	dean–deal

Overheard in the South:
"The raison ah don't want y'all to lane on mah shoulder is that ah have a cold. Hand me a clinics, and I'll mate you later."

Try it this way: "The reason I don't want you to lean on my shoulder is that I have a cold. Hand me a Kleenex, and I'll meet you later."

4. For ee: The tongue is high and far forward.

If this sound bugs you, tape yourself as you read the following. Be sure your friend listens to you. It's often surprisingly tough for you to tell yourself if you're substituting another sound for ee.

If you're permitting an illicit uh to elbow its way in, these sentences will also give you a good workout:

> Whenever I get eager and feel like exercise, I lie down till the feeling passes.
>
> Please, Lord, teach me so that my words will be easy, tender, and sweet, for tomorrow I may have to eat them.
>
> Few really believe. Most only believe that they believe or even make believe.
>
> Sleep faster. We need the pillow.
> [Yiddish proverb]
>
> If you're angry—speak. You'll make the best speech you'll ever regret.
>
> A person always has two reasons for doing anything—a good reason and the real reason.

i

Example   A baby-sitter is not experienced until she knows which kid to sit with and which kid to sit on.

How to . . .   Say the ee of meet. Now, lower your tongue slightly and pull it back a bit as you sound the i in it. Your lips and tongue should also be more relaxed for this sound than for ee.

Faults and Foibles

5. Nonnative speakers may swap i (bit) for ee (beet). Result: Feel becomes fill; seat becomes sit.

   As you now know, for ee the tongue is high and far forward, but for i it is lower and farther back in the mouth. Feel and hear the difference as you read these:

reap–rip	keen–kin
seek–sick	deal–dill
bean–bin	seen–sin

The Spanish language doesn't contain a vowel sound exactly like the English i. Hispanics sometimes have trouble with i and substitute ee. Gyp sounds more like jeep; itch sounds more like each.

As you make the ee or i sound in the word columns below—

ee	i
Spread your lips a bit—almost smiling. Arch the blade of your tongue high in the front of your mouth. The tongue is tense.	Spread your lips slightly, but less than for ee. Your tongue is lower and more relaxed than it is for ee.

(First read down each column—then across the page.)

greet	grit
Jean	gin
wheel	will
bead	bid
cheap	chip
steal	still
Pete	pit
mead	mid

6. Don't make a major production of i. It's almost always a shorter sound than ee. If you hold onto i, you may inadvertently slip in that obtrusive uh again. Fit becomes fi-uht and Bill becomes Bi-uhl.

As you do the sentences below, cut the sound quite short. Keep it lax.

If it is to be, it's up to me.

Income: something that you can't live without or within.

Graffiti on wall of an abandoned church: We didn't invent sin. We're just trying to perfect it.

Any man who pits his intelligence against a fish and loses has it coming.

Kissing is a practice which shortens life—single life.

To feel fit as a fiddle you must tone down your middle.

e

Example A gentleman from Memphis said this about his last Las Vegas vacation: "Out by jet, back in debt."

How to . . . Let the back of your tongue touch your upper molars. The tongue tip should be behind the lower front teeth. Your jaw will drop slightly.

Faults and Foibles
"Ayd, don't forget to git some brayd and aygs." Translation: "Ed, don't forget to get some bread and eggs."

This is the kind of talk you'll hear now and then in Appalachia—a region in the eastern United States which extends roughly from southern Pennsylvania to northeastern Alabama.

Ay (rate) is substituted for e (beg).

Result: Leg and dead become layg and dayd.

In the Midwest, South, and Southwest many speakers also tend to switch i (pin) for e (beg).

Result: Ten and red become tin and rid.

7. Contrast e with ay and i in the following. Don't shuffle the sounds around.

e words	ay words	i words
Rear of tongue touches upper molars.	Tongue midhigh. Tongue muscles tense.	Front of tongue high but relaxed.
Ben	bane	bin
den	Dane	din
bet	bait	bit
sell	sale	sill

An expert is a man who has made all the mistakes which can be made in a very narrow field.

About encores: It's better that they should want and we don't play than that we should play and they don't want.

Hell: They should have an express line for people with six sins or less.

Since it is better to speak well of the dead, let's knock them while they're still alive.

It's sobering to remember that when Mendelssohn was my age, he had already been dead for ten years.
[Victor Borge]

8. You haven't forgotten those nosy nasals, have you? They're nice, congenial sounds, but they do tend to spill over into nearby vowels. E is one of the most frequently assaulted.

Run through these, and pause where you see / /.
Say:
>
> e
>
> e/ /n
>
> m/ /e/ /n

Now omit the pauses: men

Is the e sound clear and cloudless—absolutely free of nasality?

As you practice, be sure that e doesn't travel through your nose along with m, n, and ng.

> Egg: a day's adventure for a hen.
>
> Engagement ring: a test band.
>
> God helps those who help themselves.
>
> God may help those who help themselves, but the courts are rough as hell on shoplifters.
>
> Memento: the keepsake of an event, such as a hotel room Bible.
>
> Obscenity can be found in every book except the telephone directory.

GRAB BAG: REVIEW MATERIAL FOR ALL THE VIOLATED VOWELS

9. This material contains the most frequently sullied vowels: a (ask), ee (feet), i (hit), and e (bet).

> Sleeping at the wheel is a good way to keep from growing old.
>
> If the world laughs at you, laugh right back—it's as funny as you are.
>
> A tongue four inches long can kill a man six feet tall.

A baby-sitter feeds the baby at ten, twelve, and two—and herself at nine, eleven, and one.

Many of us are at the metallic age—gold in our teeth, silver in our hair, and lead in our pants.

Let us so live that when we come to die even the undertaker will be sorry.

Fill what's empty. Empty what's full. And scratch where it itches.

Some people say that the squeaky wheel gets the grease, but others point out that it's the first one to be replaced.

A real friend will tell you when you have spinach stuck in your teeth.

Character is like glass. Even a little crack shows.

If you think a seat belt is uncomfortable, you've never tried a stretcher.

Germs attack the weakest part of your body—which is the reason for head colds.

Even the best family tree has its sap.

If you can laugh at it, you can live with it.

The vanishing American is one who pays cash for everything he buys.

To the bachelor, pictures of a wedding are horror films.

Give a quack enough rope and he'll hang up a shingle.

People become well-to-do by doing what they do well.

Kissing is where two people get so close together that they can't see anything wrong with each other.

Bill Murray's ten favorite dinner guests from all history: "I realize that I might have a seating problem with this creep heap, but on the other hand, the table chit-chat would be a blast." Ivan the Terrible, Jack the Ripper, John Wilkes Booth, Adolf Hitler, Lizzie Borden, Nero, Joe Stalin, Dracula, Lady Macbeth, Charles Manson.

6
Discipline Your Diphthongs

How now, brown cow? Check your ow sound!
Say the words slowly, and you'll discover that the two vowels you're merging in each word are ah + oo as in book. Now meld ah quickly with oo, and you'll make the diphthong ow.

A diphthong is a rapid blending of two vowels into a single sound.

However, a diphthong isn't always represented by two letters in everyday spelling. The ī in night is also a diphthong. Say the sound in slow motion, and you'll hear both vowels: ah + i (as in it).
Blend the two rapidly and you'll produce ī.
There are five diphthongs in our language. Three of them are obstreperous: ī as in ice (or night), ow as in how, oi as in oil.

THE DISABLED DIPHTHONGS

ī

Example Try to be kind to everybody. You never know who might show up on the jury at your trial.

How to . . . Start out with ah. Lower your tongue to a flat position and drop your jaw quite far. Now move to the i (it) position and lift your tongue relatively high.

Faults and Foibles

You don't have to be a UN interpreter to translate the following sentences, but it would help.

> Ah fahnally opened mah ahs.
> He fahred his rahffle at the lah-uhn.
> Kah-uhl and Ahda bah-uh with lots of stah-uhl.
> "Ah'm kah-uhnd of shah-uh," said Lah-uhl.
> The qwahr sang qwah-uhtly Frahday nah-ut.

Puzzled?

Try them again. Wherever you see ah or ah-uh, substitute ī.

Southern? Southeastern? Southwestern?

Many speakers in these areas linger so long on the first vowel component—the ah—that they cheat on the second one, turning it into uh.

> like turns into lah-uhk
> dine turns into dah-uhn

In more extreme cases, the second vowel component—the ī—is allowed to evaporate entirely. We hear lahk, dahn.

If you're southern and if you want to sound northern, you may want to overhaul your ī diphthong.

1. In the following material, read across from left to right, pausing where you see dots. Make the pauses shorter as you read—with no pauses in column four. Don't emphasize one vowel at the expense of the other.

   | wah...ild | wah..ild | wah.ild | wild |
   | sah...id | sah..id | sah.id | side |

DISCIPLINE YOUR DIPHTHONGS

| ah...iz | ah..iz | ah.iz | eyes |
| mah...il | mah..il | mah.il | mile |

Don't overstress or drop either element of ī as you practice this material. And as far as the extra uh is concerned—no trespassing!

sigh	admire	buy
biceps	lie	Ina
rhyme	Bible	scion

A lie in time saves nine.

Trying to define yourself is like trying to bite your own teeth.

Don't wait for pie in the sky when you die! Get yours now, with ice cream on top.

No matter which side of an argument you're on, you always find quite a few people on your side that you wish were on the other side.

The fly that doesn't want to be swatted is most secure when it lights on the fly swatter.

ow

Example When you're down and out, lift up your head and shout, "I'm down and out!"

How to . . . Start again with the ah position. Your tongue should be fairly low and your lips unrounded. Then as you move toward the position for oo (book), elevate your tongue and round your lips.

Faults and Foibles
Don't sound like Lena the Hyena or Yowling Yasha!
In certain sections of the East, notably in the New York

City, Philadelphia, and Baltimore areas, as well as a few scattered regions in the South, ow is often made into an extremely piercing, hooty sound which is as subtle as a dentist's drill. Instead of using *ah* as the first vowel element, many speakers from these areas use the brittle *a* of as or the *e* of egg rather than the more tender, pleasing *ah*.

Either combination—a + oo—produces an ugly, scraggy sound. And it can happen to you if your tongue is raised too high or held too tensely. A stiff jaw will also give this diphthong a vinegary edginess.

2. Once more into the breach!
Say How now, brown cow? again.
Are you making svelte and refined ow sounds? Let's double check to make certain that your diphthong isn't tainted and tinny. As you read the material below, painstakingly avoid *a* (ask) or *e* (egg) as the first vowel element of the *ou* or *ow* blends. Always start out with that amiable and docile ah of calm.

scout	tower	outrage
owl	louse	scowl
devout	country	foul

Outer space: our largest suburb.

Live around wolves and you'll soon learn how to howl.

A mousetrap: easy to enter but not so easy to get out of.

By the time you know what it's all about, it's about over.

Holding down public office is like dancing on a crowded dance floor. No matter how you move around, you're bound to rub someone the wrong way.

oi

Example   Many have pointed out that boys will be boys, but they don't have to be the James Boys.

How to ...   Start the sound from the position you use to say awe. Then let your tongue glide effortlessly to the position for i (it). Your lips are minimally rounded.

Faults and Foibles

Annoys is defined by some New Yorkers as the lady who checks your pulse in the hospital.

"The beautiful goil with the poils on toity-toid street" type of speech in the New York City area isn't quite as common as non-New Yorkers like to think. But it does show up. And some citizens of the Big Apple pronounce "girl" without an r: "ge-il."

And the same beautiful goil—with or without the poils—may drive her car into a soivice station to have her erl checked. But her cousin, a Dallas debutante, may ask the attendant to check the all in her Ferrari.

In some provincial or countrified speech, ī replaces oi. The friendly mountain folk of West Virginia, for example, may readily ask you to jine instead of join them.

3. If you've been told that your oi is quaint, rustic, or otherwise attention-getting, rehearse the drill material below.

    For comparison and contrast, read the following words across the page. Most problems with oi result from too much lip rounding. Remember that as you say oi, your lips should move from a slightly rounded to a relaxed and unrounded position.

boil	Burl	bile	ball	boil
foil	furl	file	fall	foil
loin	learn	line	lawn	loin

As soon as you feel that you have a stable and unblemished oi, read these.

loiter	void	royal	gargoyle
toyed	point	foist	choice
doily	buoy	foyer	poignant

What kind of a noise annoys a foiled oyster?

The biggest difference between men and boys is the cost of their toys.

If oil spoils water, perhaps the answer to oil spills is to paper-train the oil tankers.

There's many a boy here today who looks on war with great joy, but, boys, it is all hell.

Airplane fares have increased considerably. Even the cost of going up is going up.

GRAB BAG: REVIEW MATERIAL FOR ALL THE DISABLED DIPHTHONGS

4. This material contains the most frequently defiled diphthongs: $\bar{\text{i}}$ (ice), ow (how), oi (oil).

In baiting a mousetrap with cheese, always leave room for the mouse.

Most of the time I don't have much fun. The rest of the time I don't have any fun at all. [Woody Allen]

I think it is better to be one-sided than no-sided.

Small children, small joys; big children, big annoys.

The important thing is not to let oneself be poisoned. Hatred poisons.

The devil doesn't know how to sing, only how to howl.

When a person is down in the world, an ounce of help is better than a pound of preaching.

If you like it, they don't have it in your size. If you like it and it's in your size, it doesn't fit. If you like it and it fits, you can't afford to buy it. If you like it, it fits, and you can afford to buy it, it falls apart the first time you try to wear it.

The U.S. Congress can be divided into three categories: those who have gone out of their minds, those who are about to go out of their minds, and those who have no minds to go out of.

I went to a fight the other night and a hockey game broke out.

Snoring sounds like an open throttled Mack truck halfway up a mountain.

It's much wiser to love thy neighbor than his wife.

Life's what's important. Walking, houses, family. Birth and pain and joy—and then dying. Acting is just standing around waiting for a custard pie. That's what it's all about. [Katharine Hepburn]

How come they always tell you how the weather is at the airport but not at the busstop?

Four-word story of failure: Hired, tired, mired, fired.

It's funny how a bottle of brew can lead to bubble, bubble, toil, and trouble.

How can you rejoice, if you've never joiced? How can you be rebuked if you've never been buked? How can you reconnoiter, if you've never connoitered?

There's no harm in talking to yourself, but try to avoid telling yourself jokes you've heard before.

Let's have a merry journey, and shout about how light is good and dark is not. What we should do is not future ourselves so much. We should now ourselves more. "Now thyself" is more important than "know thyself." Get high on now. Now is wonderful. Enjoy now.

7
Speak Up!

"Sorry, can't hear you!"
"What did you say?"
"Would you speak a little louder, please?"
How often do people say these to you?
So you turn up your volume. Or maybe you just think you do. How well *does* your voice carry?

1. Let's test it. Say the line below, pretending that you're in three different situations, using three levels of loudness:

   I refuse to listen to you.
   Level 1. Say it quietly—just above a whisper. **(Soft)**
   Level 2. Casually, face to face. **(Medium loud)**
   Level 3. Vigorously. **(Loud)**
   How did you do?

Level 3 should have been about three times as loud as Level 1!

It's impossible for you to judge your own levels of loudness. Your voice is amplified by the bones in your skull, and it always sounds louder to you than to others. Anyway, you know what you're thinking, so why shouldn't you know what you're saying?

Once again, borrow a buddy or an unflappable friend and let this person do the judging. Read the Poe selection at the indicated levels of loudness. Ideally, tape it, but do *not* adjust the volume level on the recorder while reading.

(Level 1: Soft) No doubt I now grew very pale. But I talked more fluently and with a heightened voice. Yet the sound increased—and what could I do? It was a low, dull, quick sound—much such a sound as a watch makes when enveloped in cotton. I gasped for breath. Yet the officers didn't hear it. I talked more quickly, more vehemently, but the noise steadily increased. **(Level 2: Medium loud)** Oh God! What could I do? I foamed—I raved—I swore! I swung the chair upon which I had been sitting, and grated it upon the boards, but the noise arose overall and continually increased. It grew louder—louder—louder! And still the men chatted pleasantly, and smiled. Was it possible they didn't hear? Almighty God!—no, no! They heard! They suspected! They knew! **(Level 3: Loud)** They were making a mockery of my horror! But anything was better than this agony! Anything was more tolerable than this derision! I could bear those hypocritical smiles no longer! I felt that I must scream or die! And now—again! Louder! Louder! "Villains!" I shrieked, "I admit the deed! Tear up the planks! Here, here! It is the beating of his hideous heart!"

(Poe, "The Tell-Tale Heart")

Two questions for you:

Did you read the Level 3 material without yelling until you were purple in the face?

Would your Level 3 material get across in a large room or auditorium? Make an educated guess.

If the answer to both questions is yes, skip to Exercise 12.

If the answer to either or both questions is no, continue reading:

MEET INAUDIBLE INGA AND WHISPERY WILBUR

It's an ear-opening experience to attend some public meetings and listen to Inaudible Inga and Whispery Wilbur trying to get in their "two-bits worth" from the floor.

You listen, but you don't hear. A startling number of these well-intentioned mutterers seem unable to speak up! Their problem is not weakness, but lack of experience. They can't comprehend that a voice which is puny and shrunken receives little or no attention.

Sh-h-h-h-h!

Inaudible Inga and Whispery Wilbur, from the ages of two to twenty, have been programmed to turn down the volume. Urban living for many means growing up in an environment of apartments or condominiums. And screaming youngsters constantly shushed by their parents eventually respond by reducing their loudness levels to vocalized whispers. Another bad habit is launched.

By the time Inga and Wilbur reach adulthood, they're apparently unable to talk any louder.

Mental blocks? Possibly.

Inga and Wilbur don't want to hear themselves any louder.

No Chutzpa, Please!

Inga's own personal code of behavior dictates that a quiet, gentle speaking level is ideal. To her, loudness is noise pollution, and it's associated with aggressive, even obnoxious behavior. Extroverts are always loudmouths, thinks Inga. Sometimes they are.

And Wilbur doesn't want to speak in a way that conflicts with his self-image. He's a gentleman, and gentlemen don't raise their voices.

In both cases, shyness or reserve may also be responsible for their faint and fragile voices.

And something else—they may react to the noisy, blaring, and raucous world around them by turning down their own volume. Radios and record players simultaneously doing rock and Rachmaninoff (full blast), TV sets, low-flying 747s, Yamaha bikes, souped-up cars with exploding mufflers, sirens, bells, and whistles. And always the yells, grunts, gurgles, squeaks, and squawks of the human sonic boom.

Inga and Wilbur gave up a long time ago. Can you blame them? Under some circumstances silence apparently is the best solution.

But talking too softly suggests that you're insecure and unsure of yourself. And what's worse—it signals hearers that you don't genuinely believe in what you're saying. If people can't hear you, you'll quickly be forgotten. You'll be passed over. You'll become an "also-ran."

PROJECT!

A bride tosses her bouquet. Customarily, she throws it in the general direction of the bridesmaids, but not necessarily at a specific woman. A baseball pitcher throws a ball, but aims it in the direction of a specific individual—the catcher.

If we speak of loudness, we are, in a sense, "tossing" the voice in a general direction with sufficient strength and power so that most of those present can hear and understand what we are saying. If we speak of projection, we are beaming the voice to a particular group or to a rather specific area.

Projection is controlled energy that gives impact and intelligibility to sound. It involves a deliberate concentration and a strong desire to communicate with your listeners.

Have you ever attended a play produced in theater-in-the-round, arena, or central staging? The audience is often seated on four sides of a central playing area. This means that regardless of where an actor stands, some part of the audience cannot see the actor's face. But the performer who projects can be easily heard and understood by all segments of the audience.

How To Project with Pep, Push, and Punch

Open Your Mouth!
Your voice doesn't carry if it doesn't have much chance to get out of your mouth in the first place!

2. Try the old tongue twister "Peter Piper picked a peck of pickled peppers" three ways:

>Say it as if your lips are glued together and your jaw wired shut.
>Say it with normal lip and jaw activity.
>Open your mouth as widely as you can. *Grimace!*
>(Don't try to look pretty.)

Can you feel and hear the differences?

Speak Sounds That Are Spirited and Springy!
The blond fox of Oz said, "Gosh!" as he squashed the kumquat. Practice this and the nonsense material below. You'll quickly discover that loudness alone won't put it over. You'll be compelled to fatten your vowels and diphthongs and, above all, to tackle your consonants with force and accuracy.

Your primary target with the jabberwocky below is the gusty and gutsy projection of speech sounds.

3. Read these energetically:

>Olive, the odd otter, sat on the oblong palm at the opera.
>Ong gnawed the eggnog in Sergeant Saul's ominous vault.

A hundred muggers threw marshmallows at Bonnie, the fluttering usher.

Cobblers often knock Tom the Jock on Wanda's yacht.

Audrey and Austin waltzed in Grandpa's long johns in Austria.

Don Juan coughed as he drank the awful coffee in Boston.

Pack the Tone From the Guts.

A burly and seasoned marine sergeant whose job was teaching potential drill instructors once told me: "I don't tell 'em anything scientific about shoutin' commands. I just tell 'em to pack the tone from the guts. And it works!"

It probably does, too.

To put it more delicately, however, the sergeant was advising his students to get their propulsive power from their midregions. The strength and vitality that produce loud, firm tones *come from the muscles of breathing, mostly in the middle areas of your body*, and not from the muscles of your throat.

4. Give these commands some clout. Say them briskly but keep the throat as relaxed as possible. Notice the sudden contraction of your abdominal muscles as you project the phrases.

All aboard	All ashore!
Ship ahoy!	On the double!
Ready! Aim! Fire!	Stop, or I'll shoot!
Hands up!	Open in the name of the law!

Vitalize Your Vowels, Dust Off Your Diphthongs

"Speak slower!"

Marvelous advice, and most of us pay as much attention

to it as we do to "Drive carefully!" If you're told to slow down while you're talking, what you probably do is put longer pauses between words and phrases. (Try producing a loud pause and see what comes out.)

As far as loudness is concerned, what "Speak slower!" really means is slowing down on the words. Point up your vowels and diphthongs by hanging onto and stre-e-e-etching them. *They* are the sounds that cut through.

Say "stop!" You can make a lot more of the right kind of noise on the **o** than you can on the **st—p**.

5. Try a hale and hardy approach with the following. The dashes will remind you to le-e-engthen your vowels and diphthongs. Exaggerate.

O-u-t, da-amned spo-ot, o-u-t, I-I sa-ay!

Loo-ook too-oo thi-is day-ay! Fo-or i-it i-is the ve-ery wa-ay o-of li-ife!

Go-old! Go-old! Go-old! Bri-ight a-and ye-ellow-ow, ha-ard a-and co-old!

Whe-en i-in dou-oubt, do-on't.

Whe-en I-Irish e-eyes a-are smi-iling, wa-atch yo-our ste-ep!

May-ay the de-evil cha-ase you-ou e-every day-ay o-of you-our li-ife a-and ne-ever ca-atch you-ou.

Zip Along With Zest—Be Dynamic!

Are you vocally pallid? Indifferent?

If somebody makes you speak louder, do you protest: "But I'm *screaming!*"

You're *not* screaming!

If your mental and physical health is good, you'll have sockeroo projection if you speak with more beef and brawn. Your entire body must respond! A well-projected voice doesn't merely reach its hearers, it penetrates them. Animation and power are there for the asking if you have something to say, a purpose in saying it and, above all, a strong desire to say it.

Billy Graham was asked how he attracted such mammoth audiences and held them spellbound. "I set myself on fire," he replied, "and they come to watch me burn!"

Project at a Proper Pitch level.

"Speak Low" is a smart song title, and it's good advice if you're lucky enough to own a naturally deep voice.

But it's not so good if you're trying to produce the "voice-from-the-mummy's-tomb" and speaking at a level that's too low for you. Or if you're a soprano who lets your voice soar into outer space, you may be speaking (or squeaking?) at a pitch level that is too high for you.

In either case, the resulting sound is generally terrible. And talking this way can also be dangerous for your voice and throat.

Both of the extremes—too low or too high—often go hand-in-hand with underprojection.

Do you have two speaking voices?

Even if you're using your most effective pitch level in everyday conversation, what happens if you're faced with an emergency and have to yell for help? Your pitch may sneak upward five or six tones.

Geraldine Ferraro has a Dr. Jekyll-Mrs. Hyde voice. In informal situations, her voice is nicely pitched. But with a forest of mikes and a large audience in front of her, she tends to become ear-piercing.

6. Pretend that you're in a large room with 300 people. Say "Halt! Who goes there?" three times:

   The first time, say it to the people in the front row.

   The second time, speak to the people in the middle of the room—about twenty-five feet away.

   The third time, aim it at the audience in the rear of

SPEAK UP!

the room—fifty feet from you.
Each time you say the phrase:

- Keep your throat relaxed.
- Let your abdominal muscles give you the extra push.
- Don't let your pitch zoom upward! Use approximately the same pitch level for the third time as you used for the first.

7. Begin ah softly, and then increase it to your loudest tone of good quality. Hold the loud tone for a few seconds, and then decrease it to your softest tone of satisfactory quality. Repeat several times. *Keep that pitch constant!*
8. Hold ah at a respectable pitch level for about five seconds. Keep the throat open and the pitch steady. Avoid strain. Then try it at three levels of loudness, using the pattern suggested in Exercise 6.
9. Musicians are concerned with signs and symbols as well as notes. The sign < indicates a gradual increase in loudness (a crescendo). The sign > indicates a gradual decrease in loudness (a decrescendo). Borrowing these convenient signs, read the material as indicated:

a. <

ABCDEFG

b. >

HIJKLMN

c.

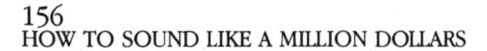

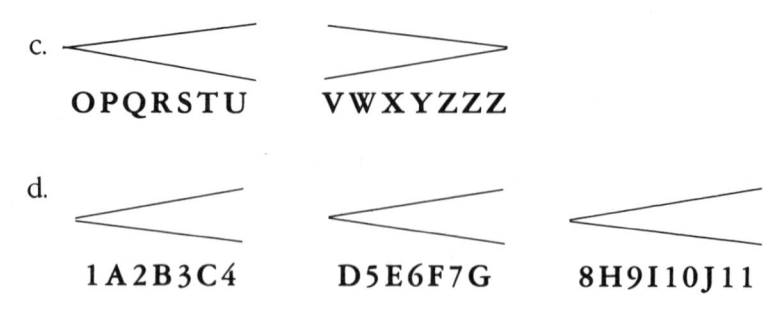

OPQRSTU   VWXYZZZ

d.

1A2B3C4   D5E6F7G   8H9I10J11

VOCAL SUICIDE: HOW TO EVADE AND AVOID IT

Going to a sports event or a rock concert?

What you'll probably do there is bellow at three levels: loud, louder, and LOUDEST.

And then—Monday morning! Your throat is raw and inflamed, and your voice—what is left of it—is croaky and hoarse. It hurts to talk. You blame your sore throat on the excessive whooping, shrug it off, and assume that in a day or two the rawness will disappear.

If you indulge in this excessive noisemaking only occasionally, it probably won't do any permanent damage. But too much screaming can harm your vocal apparatus. The vocal cords may rub or bump together and, in time, small knobs known as vocal nodes, or screamer's nodules, may develop. If this happens to you, you'll be visiting your local laryngologist, tracheotomist, or otorhinolaryngologist—medical doctors who are primarily interested in your throat or larynx. Surgery is often necessary.

Vocal hangovers aren't confined to sports or rock fans. Lawyers, teachers, actors, and speakers—more often the green, inexperienced novice than the seasoned professional—can be victims of acute hoarseness.

On the other hand, there are thousands of individuals who don't develop hoarseness even though their jobs or professions require them to speak loudly enough to be heard successfully over relatively large areas and not always with the help of a microphone. Broadway stars must get their voices across to audiences as often as eight times a week for months on end. Clergy, lawyers, politicians—seldom do these individuals suffer from overstrained voices. The logical conclusion: It's the quality, not the quantity, of loudness that causes huskiness.

In this chapter I'm trying to help you build a voice that is sufficiently loud and varied for most normal speaking situations rather than showing you how to howl and yowl at football games. A well-projected voice is not hooting and hollering!

As a switch, let's go for four levels of loudness:

soft
    medium loud
        LOUD
            VERY LOUD

Shying away from that fourth level—VERY LOUD? Don't.

Keep this uppermost in mind: Loudness is a *relative* term. There are, for example, at least four different kinds of VERY LOUD:

soft VERY LOUD
    medium loud VERY LOUD
        LOUD VERY LOUD
            VERY LOUD VERY LOUD

10. Read across the columns of words at the four levels, doing the same four words on one breath.

    A little bodily activity will help you. Make two fists, and as you say each word, punch out straight ahead of you. The louder the word the bigger your punch. Sound silly? It works! Try it.

HOW TO SOUND LIKE A MILLION DOLLARS

soft	medium loud	*LOUD*	VERY LOUD
hey	hey	*HEY*	HEY
leave	leave	*LEAVE*	LEAVE
out	out	*OUT*	OUT
boo	boo	*BOO*	BOO

11. The instructions in parentheses suggest a loudness level for these shorties:

(Telephone conversation; quiet) I'll see you in five minutes.

(Casual, face-to-face) That doctor's a quack.

(Vigorous) You know better than that!

(Powerful determination) You can't get away with this!

As you read these, repeat the pattern suggested in the first part of the exercise.

I have no idea where she is.
Let's go on a picnic tonight.
He always cheats at cards.
I've never been so mad!

Sorry, but I'm busy tonight.
Sorry, but I'm busy tonight.
Sorry, but I'm busy tonight.
Sorry, but I'm busy tonight.

I haven't seen you in months.
Why is that card up your sleeve?
I don't care what you think.
I don't care what anyone thinks.

You've said that a hundred times.
I'll never wait for you again.
Don't bother me. Let me alone!
Listen to me. We're all through!

12. Can you borrow a large room, gym, auditorium, or Radio City Music Hall for this exercise? Take a buddy. Have your audience of one seated as far away from you as possible.

Read each sentence at the four loudness levels. Your private audience may not hear the first two levels as easily as the last two, but if you're giving your performance some moxie, you'll find that even a whisper can be heard fifty feet away.

DON'TS AND DOS

- DON'T let your voice take off like a skyrocket.
- DO speak at a suitable general pitch level and stay there.
- DON'T get your support from your throat.
- DO get your pushing power from your midregion.
- DON'T tighten up.
- DO loosen up.
- DON'T compress the accented vowels and diphthongs.
- DO expand them.

Cry "God for Harry, England, and Saint George!"

A horse! A horse! My kingdom for a horse!

A Yankee ship and a Yankee crew! Ye ho, ye hoo! Ye ho, ye hoo!

Come live, be merry, and join with me to swing the sweet chorus of "Ha, ha, ha!"

Who cares for nothing alone is free—sit down, good friends, and drink with me!

Fifteen men on the dead man's chest—yo-ho-ho, and a bottle of rum!

WHEN TO PURR, WHEN TO ROAR, AND WHAT TO DO IN BETWEEN

Composer Franz Joseph Haydn worked a charming stunt into his Surprise Symphony. Fearing that the audience might snooze during the quiet section of the work, he inserted several extremely loud, crashing chords where they would be least expected. "That's sure to make them jump," he is supposed to have said.

And jump they did!

Your vocal volume has to be sufficiently high-powered so that your listeners can hear you. But it must also be adapted to the situation. Don't turn up your volume in a coffee, cocktail, or Coors conversation as much as you would if you were talking to 30 or 300 people in a large room. An orchestra never plays so loudly that it blasts the audience out of the concert hall; it never plays so quietly that the audience can't hear it. But within those limits, it plays at different levels of loudness as the music—and the acoustics of the hall—dictate.

A final word about loudness: Be prepared for competition. Wherever you're talking, you may have to contend with noise around you: gabby people, banging air conditioners, and the racket from the outside world. Rise above it! Adjust your volume accordingly.

8
Be Vibrant, Varied, Vivid and Versatile!

> Now I lay me down to sleep,
> The lecture dull, the subject deep;
> If he should quit before I wake,
> Give me a poke, for heaven's sake!
> [Anonymous]

That three word phrase at the beginning of the second line, *The lecture dull*, is a key to what this chapter is about.

Vocal monotony is a plague that strikes clergy, lawyers, nurses, legislators, astronauts, housepersons, students, butchers, bakers, and candlestick-makers! Nobody's immune.

THE DRONE'S GALLERY:

Sluggish Sylvester thinks slowly, moves slowly, and talks slowly.

Shy Sheila is self-conscious, shrinking, and sheepish.

Languid Lester is lethargic, listless, and lazy.

Dejected Debbie is depressed, despondent, or down-in-the-mouth.

Chilly Charlie is cold-hearted, cold-blooded, and callous.

Denny Dimwit is dense, dopey, and dead.

Do *you*, by any remote chance, belong to the Drone's Gallery? (Maybe you're just a part-time monotone.) No one likes to be tagged as drab, dismal, or droopy!

HOW TO SOUND LIKE A MILLION DOLLARS

CLEAN OUT THOSE COBWEBS

Make a realistic attempt to face the problem head-on. The old saw, "The leopard can't change his spots," is quite true—for leopards. If you're receptive as you work on the material in this chapter, you'll remove yourself from the Drone's Gallery, or the part-time monotone's category (and enjoy yourself in the process!).

If you have a chance, listen to Henry Kissinger, former Secretary of State. Gloomy, grave, and grimy: a painful drone. The drone typically reads or talks using a skimpy, shrivelled range of two to four tones.

People with glimmer and shimmer in their voices have a range of twelve to fourteen tones!

The next few exercises will help you remove the rust and dust from the upper and lower extremes of your range. Or they'll show you how to use expressively and flexibly the range you already have.

1. Hum a tone that is easy and comfortable for you. From there, hum down the scale to your lowest safe tone. Don't scrape rock bottom. Then hum back up the scale to your highest decent tone, and don't strain at the top. You'll most likely discover that your range is about twelve tones and possibly more.

2. Do a vocal walk *up* the scale. Say the first word in each line on a comfortably low pitch, and pitch each succeeding word a half or a whole tone higher.

> Sink or swim.
>
> Long tongues: short friendships.
>
> Little things affect little minds.
>
> That most knowing of persons—gossip.
>
> Cigarettes are killers that travel in packs.
>
> The Bible promises no loaves to the loafer.

BE VIBRANT, VARIED, VIVID AND VERSATILE!

Many a bee has drowned in his own honey.

It is better to wear out than to rust out.

Did the devil really create the world when God wasn't looking?

How awful to reflect that what people say of us is true.

It pays to keep your feet on the ground, but keep them moving.

It seems sort of significant that we have two ears and only one mouth.

Love is a battle, love is a war; above all, love is a growing up.

A drunkard can't make both ends meet because he's much too busy making one end drink.

Diet: a system of starving yourself to death just so that you can live a little longer.

If ants are such busy little workers, how come they find time to go to all the picnics?

A doctor is a person who tells you that if you don't cut out something, he will.

3. Repeat Exercise 2, but this time do your vocal walk *down* the scale. Say the first word on a comfortably high pitch, and pitch each succeeding word a half or a whole tone lower.

4. Singers commonly use a warming-up exercise that is also helpful in developing flexible range. To sing a scale, you would sing "do re me fa sol la ti do" (or if it is easier, "one two three four five six seven eight"). In this exercise use only "do me sol do" ("one three five eight").

   Do this exercise many times, and experiment by placing the first note on different tones.

GIVE YOUR VOICE SOME GET-UP-AND-GO!

Here are a few techniques that will add color and razzle-dazzle to your speaking. The most trivial, lackluster subjects can be made exciting if you use these techniques. This is important, because so much of our daily conversation is about piddling, commonplace subjects.

Key is the general pitch level—ranging anywhere from high to low—that is used at any given moment in talking or reading.

If you win your state's $2,000,000 lottery, you'll report your good news to the world in a **high key.** Even if you don't luck out, and are simply saying or reading something that is light, humorous, or cheerful, your key will be in the higher part of your range.

The zany trial scene from *Alice in Wonderland*, in which the Queen of Hearts shouts, "Sentence first. Verdict afterwards. Off with his head!" is most convincing in a high key.

Catch a few TV commercials (can they be avoided?), and you'll note that many of the performers do their stuff in a comparatively high key: "Now that you've just seen how truly fast and deadly Mother Poppins's bug-killer is, why don't you rush out immediately and buy a case or two for your home?"

On the negative side, the voices of people in a rage or scared spitless also often soar into the upper regions.

If you talk about a recent shopping trip, a vacation at Yellowstone National Park, or a date, you'll probably use a **middle key.** Informal, casual, and unemotional ideas or material work best in this middle range.

But if you tell somebody about the death of a friend, if you're feeling romantic under a full moon, or if you're digging deeply into Nietzsche, you'll use a **low key.** Quiet, melancholy, or profound ideas tend to seek out the lower depths.

General Douglas MacArthur's classic speech to Congress

in 1951 had the entire nation dissolved in tears. In his closing sentences, he carefully shifted to a low key: "Old soldiers never die; they just fade away. I now close my military career . . . an old soldier who tried to do his duty as God gave him to see that duty. Good-bye."

5. Read these selections in a **high key.** But don't deliver them in a high monotone. Work for contrast, color, and variation within that area.

> Know thyself. A Yale undergraduate left on his door a note for a friend on which was written, "Call me at seven o'clock; it is absolutely necessary that I get up at seven. Make no mistake. Keep knocking until I answer." Under this he had written: "Try again at ten."
>
> I'm tired of all this nonsense about beauty being only skin-deep. That's deep enough. What do you want—an adorable liver? If you are a miracle of beauty, you can't help it. That's why you are so much applauded for it.
> [Farrah Fawcett]
>
> Love makes you feel special. It changes everyone for the better. It's the one commodity that multiplies when you give it away. The more you spread it around, the more you are able to hang on to it because it keeps coming back to you. Where love is concerned, it pays to be an absolute spend-thrift. It can't be bought or sold, so throw it away! Splash it all over! Empty your pockets! Shake the basket! Turn it upside down! Shower it on everyone—even those who don't deserve it! You may startle them into behaving in a way you never dreamed possible. Not only is it the great mystery of life, it's also the most powerful motivator known to mankind.
>
> I'll do the explaining, Sir! When the war began, like the dutiful wives we are, we tolerated you men,

and endured your actions in silence. Small wonder. You wouldn't let us say boo. We'd sit at home, and we'd hear that you men had done it again—mishandled another big issue with your staggering incompetence. Then, masking our worry with a nervous laugh, we'd ask you: "And did you manage to end the war in the assembly this morning?" And what did you say to us? "What's it to you? Shut up!" Now we women are going to set you right! Inside there we have four battalions—fully armed fighting women completely equipped for war. What did you expect? We're not slaves. We're freedom women, and when we're scorned, we're full of fury. Never underestimate the power of a woman! Into the fray! Smash them to bits! The day is ours! [Aristophanes, *Lysistrata*]

6. Read these selections in a **middle key.** Again, strive for flexibility and variety.

I'm cheerful. I'm not happy, but I'm cheerful. There's a big difference. A happy woman has no cares at all; a cheerful woman has cares and learns to ignore that.

[Beverly Sills]

The Statue of Liberty: made by an Italian, presented to the American people on behalf of the French government for the purpose of welcoming Irish immigrants to New York, which was founded by Dutch people who had stolen it from the Indians and in which today's largest ethnic group is Jewish.

When I was a boy of fourteen, my father was so ignorant I could hardly stand to have the old man around. But when I got to be twenty-one, I was amazed at how much he had learned in seven years. [Mark Twain]

The crowd cheered lustily as the team trotted on the field. Eleven mighty and determined men

BE VIBRANT, VARIED, VIVID AND VERSATILE!

going forth to fight for the old alma mater, to give their all. With them came Charlie. Everybody knew Charlie. On the campus his bubbling personality had won him many friends. He turned and faced the fans. He grinned. There was confidence as well as determination in his grin. He assumed the pose the vast crowd had seen so often. With an assured tone in his voice he barked out, "Peanuts, popcorn, candy!"

7. Read these selections in a **low key,** but don't freeze your voice at one level. Let it rise and fall.

> Today marks my final roll call with you. But I want you to know that when I cross the river, my last conscious thoughts will be of the Corps, and the Corps, and the Corps. I bid you farewell.
> [Douglas MacArthur]

> The day is cold, and dark, and dreary,
> It rains, and the wind is never weary;
> The vine still clings to the mouldering wall,
> But at every gust the dead leaves fall,
> And the day is dark and dreary.

> ... Yea, though I walk through the valley of the shadow of death, I will fear no evil; for thou art with me. Thy rod and thy staff they comfort me. Thou preparest a table before me in the presence of mine enemies; thou anointest my head with oil. My cup runneth over. Surely goodness and mercy shall follow me all the days of my life, and I will dwell in the house of the Lord forever.
> [The Twenty-Third Psalm]

> What is the most famous monument ever built in honor of love? The incomparable Taj Mahal—a shimmering, white jewel that seems to float over the hot Indian plain. It is a tomb, and it tells one of the greatest love stories of all time. A great shah, when he was only nineteen, fell in love with a highborn beauty and married her.

She gave the shah many children. She ruled at his side as an equal. He adored her and brought her diamonds and flowers. In the tenth year of their marriage, once again she was with child, but this time, something strange occurred. She confided that shortly before the baby was born, she heard it cry in her womb—an ill omen. A healthy baby girl was born, but the queen did not recover. As she lay dying, she whispered a final wish to her grief-stricken husband: "Build for me a monument so pure and perfect that anyone who comes to it will feel the great power of love." She paused and then added, "... and the even greater power of death."

8. Which key—**high, middle,** or **low**—is most appropriate for each of the following? Experiment by trying the selections in more than one key. Be as expressive as you can.

>I am thy father's spirit, doomed for a certain time to walk the night.
>
>Why condemn the devil? He's using the same defense many of us are using: "I'm doing my own thing."
>
>If you have to kiss somebody at 7 A.M. in front of the camera, you'd better be friends. [Liza Minelli]
>
>We are such stuff as dreams are made of and our little life is rounded with a sleep.
>
>The hardest thing any person can do is to fall down on the ice when it's slippery, and then get up and praise the Lord.
>
>If at first you don't succeed, try, try again. Then quit. There's no use being a damn fool about it.

SLIDE AND GLIDE

Changing pitch within a single, uninterrupted sound is called an inflection.

BE VIBRANT, VARIED, VIVID AND VERSATILE!

A **rising inflection** is an upward gliding of the voice from a low to a high pitch. Say:

w-h-o?

The upward slide indicates questioning, hesitancy, curiosity, suspense, surprise, perplexity.

A **falling inflection** is a downward gliding of the voice from a high to a low pitch. Say:

n-o-w!

The downward slide denotes certainty, command, emphasis, finality.

A double inflection combines the upward and downward gliding of the voice. Say:

o-h-h-h!

The double inflection signifies uncertainty, sarcasm, evasion, double or hidden meanings.

9. Read each of these words three times using a rising, a falling, and then a double inflection. Exaggerate your inflections.

ah	yes	now	don't
hey	well	please	maybe
no	why	good	here

10. Experiment with the inflections and say oh, suggesting these meanings:

elation	sarcasm	indifference
fear	doubt	finality

HOW TO SOUND LIKE A MILLION DOLLARS

    pity   anger   curiosity
    amazement disgust   bashfulness

11. Try each of these words aloud, using a suitable inflection. The sentence in parentheses suggests a specific meaning for the word, but don't read the sentence aloud.

    So (We've caught you at last, you rascal!)
    So (What's it to you?)

    Jim (Is that you tiptoeing upstairs?)
    Jim (What do you mean by coming in at this hour?)

    Why (I've never heard of such a thing.)
    Why (I'll tell you why.)

    Wow (Isn't it a beauty?)
    Wow (I've had it!)

    Really (Did it actually happen?)
    Really (Don't ever speak to me again.)

    Help (I'm drowning!)
    Help (Why should I?)

HOP, SKIP, AND JUMP!

A pitch change between words or syllables is known as a step. The voice leaps or springs from one pitch to another, either up or down. Only one tone is used per word.

12. In these sentences the position of the word indicates the location of the step and the relative size of the jump. Imagine the words on a musical staff.

```
        you
            say                    I'll
                that                   scream.
                    again
If
```

BE VIBRANT, VARIED, VIVID AND VERSATILE!

---

       now
            forever
                 hold
Speak   your
        or   peace.

   I
      do   do
              it
If
    say   it,   fast.

---

                           mean?
                    you
               what
         to understand
    supposed
  I
Am

Smile,
              that,
     when you say
                my friend!

Karen,
            me?
      marry
   will you

Oh,   never
   John, you and I   get
              would   along!

HOW TO SOUND LIKE A MILLION DOLLARS

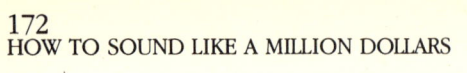

```
           that                     not
Don't try       again,                  kidding!
                    Jack,       I'm
                          and
```

```
Care-                     near-
    ful!                      er.
           They're getting        Oops!
                                      It's
                                          too
                                              late.
```

---

13. Look over these sentences and experiment with a pattern of keys, inflections, and steps that fits the general meaning of each line. Then read the material aloud.

>Mark, I hate to do this. Here's your ring.

>Strange—that I should run into her every place I go.

>He's such a nerd—how much money did you say he inherited?

>Oh, Charles, a mink coat! It's just what I wanted!

>I'm tired, I'm sick, I'm disgusted, and I'm boiling mad!

>Helen, is that you? Why, Mabel, what are you doing here?

>Judy? Didn't you know? She died more than three years ago.

>Who stole my billfold? Oh, here it is on the desk.

GADGETS AND GEWGAWS

Anybody can say "I'm the happiest person in the world!" choosing the proper key, the right inflections, and the most effective

BE VIBRANT, VARIED, VIVID AND VERSATILE!

steps. The sentence might be coldly correct, and yet the overall effect would still be mechanical, bland, or false. Gimmicks are helpful, but they're not quite enough. If you're inhibited, all the gadgets and gewgaws in existence won't add one iota of flash and splash to your voice.

14. As an interesting venture, read these one-liners twice. In your first reading, ignore the obvious emotional nature of the material. Deliberately give a flat and cold reading. In your second reading, respond with as much sincerity, vitality and animation as possible.

> I'm frightened
> Am I happy!
> She's dead! You're sure?
> I hate him.
> I'm sad.
>
> I'm suspicious of her.
> My, how eerie it is.
> Get out of here!
>
> You're the murderer!
> What wonderful news!
> How awful.
> Go ahead! I dare you!
> You're too late—he just died.
> I guess I'm in love.
> Please don't leave me.

UPSIE-DOWNSIE? GET OFF THE SEESAW!

Inexperienced or careless individuals are sometimes guilty of using a fixed melody pattern over and over again until it not only calls attention to itself but becomes extremely vexing to listeners.

Fond parents will pardon their fourth grader for giving a recitation on a vocal seesaw:

> Listen, my   you shall
>   children, and   hear
>   midnight   Paul Re-
> Of the   ride of   vere.

It's more difficult to excuse the clergyperson who sing-songs:

HOW TO SOUND LIKE A MILLION DOLLARS

```
                    health
              in          till
         and                  death
     sickness                      do
In                                     us part.
```

And should we be expected to forgive anyone who ends every sentence with an upward swoop?

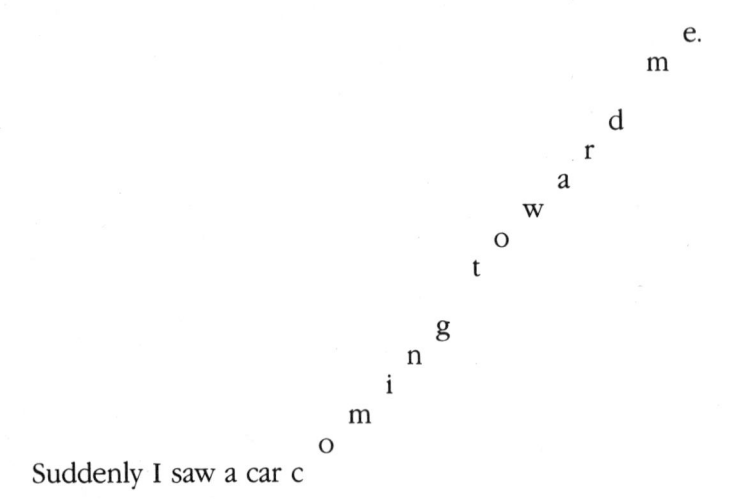

```
                              e.
                           m
                        d
                      r
                     a
                   w
                  o
                 t
              g
            n
           i
         m
        o
Suddenly I saw a car c
```

There are other repetitive patterns that are tiresome. Howard Cosell—until recently, one of the highest-paid sportscasters in the business—uses almost angular pitch patterns and turns square corners as he talks. He is an easy target for mimics and impersonators.

The late Maurice Evans was acclaimed by some for his Shakespearean interpretations. Others felt that he acted *Hamlet*, for example, as if he had mental hookworms. He chanted important, key lines as if he were bouncing a ball down the stairs:

BE VIBRANT, VARIED, VIVID AND VERSATILE!

Oh,
   that
      this
         too,
           too
              solid
                 flesh
                    would
                       melt,
                          thaw,
                            and
                              resolve
                                 itself
                                    into
                                      a
                                        dew.

If you've been accused of sing-songing or using a tired pitch pattern, listen to yourself critically. A considerable amount of work with a tape recorder is essential. As you read or speak, generally avoid using the same melody pattern on two or more consecutive phrases. Four phrases or sentences delivered in this melody pattern, for example, would be deadly.

```
 _____
|A funny thing happened   |
                     last night.

 _____
|I went out to get        |
                     a coke.

 _____
|A big man was standing in the|
                         doorway.

 _____
|I tried to get by him but he |
                         wouldn't move.
```

But four phrases or sentences delivered in varying patterns can be striking:

HOW TO SOUND LIKE A MILLION DOLLARS

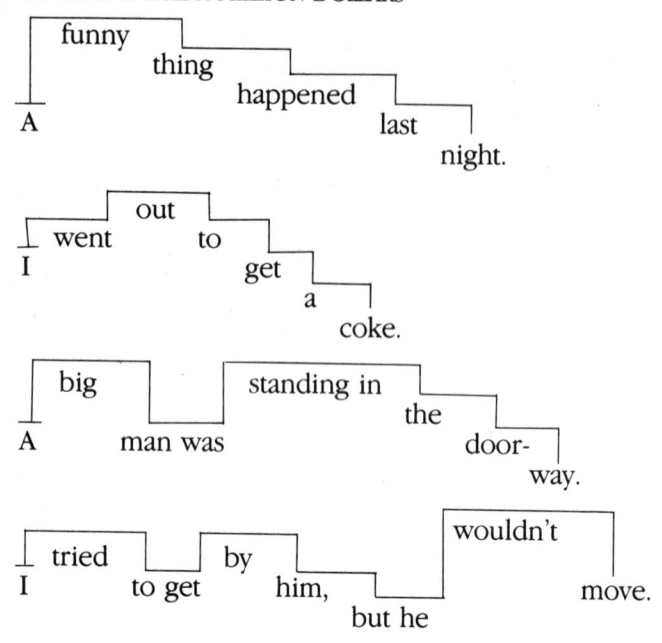

A funny thing happened last night.

I went out to get a coke.

A big man was standing in the doorway.

I tried to get by him, but he wouldn't move.

15. If you're a sing-songer or use another kind of stereotype, tape the selections below. The first time you read them, make no attempt to correct repetitive pitch patterns. Then, analyze the same selections, marking them with diagrams or lines—any of the devices used in this chapter—and work for a more subtle, imaginative melody pattern. Record and compare with your previous performance.

>Ring out, wild bells, to the wild sky,
>The flying cloud, the frosty light:
>The year is dying in the night;
>Ring out, wild bells, and let him die.
>
>Ring out the old, ring in the new,
>Ring, happy bells, across the snow:
>The year is going, let him go:
>Ring out the false, ring in the true.

Don Juan: Aha! And where did this one come from? Did you ever see anything more delightful?

Turn just a little, please. What a charming figure! Look up a little. What a pretty little face. Open your eyes wide. Aren't they beautiful? Now a glimpse of your teeth. Delicious! And what inviting lips! And a girl like you marrying a scrubby peasant? Never! You weren't born to live in the middle of a hell-hole. I've been sent here to prevent you from marrying that dolt. To get to the point. I love you with all my heart. Say the word and I'll take you away and show you the kind of life you deserve. Is my proposal rather sudden? It's your fault. You're much too beautiful. You have made me fall as deeply in love with you in a quarter of an hour as in six months with anyone else. [Molière, *Don Juan*]

Donna Elvira: For a man who is used to this sort of thing, you're certainly not very convincing, are you? I'm almost sorry to see you so embarrassed. And now the lies will start again, won't they? Why don't you swear that your feelings for me are the same as ever? Why don't you swear that you love me more than anything else in the world—'til death do us part? Oh, I'm amazed at my own stupidity! I knew what you were doing. Common sense told me you were guilty. But my simple little mind was busy inventing excuses for you. Did a day pass that you weren't with some other woman? No! You're going to be punished for what you've done to me, Don Juan. If God Himself has no terrors for you, then let me warn you. Beware the fury of a scorned woman! [Molière, *Don Juan*]

Andre: Oh, where has all my past life gone to? The time when I was young and clever, when I used to have great dreams. Why do we all become so dull and commonplace and uninteresting almost before we've begun to live? Why do we get lazy, useless, unhappy? People in this town do nothing but eat, drink, sleep. Then they die, and some more take their places, and they eat, drink, and sleep too. And they indulge in their stupid gossip and vodka and gambling. The wives deceive their husbands, and the husbands lie to their wives, and they pretend they don't see or hear anything. It's all so stupid! [Chekhov, *The Three Sisters*]

Judge Brack: There is something else, Hedda—something rather ugly. The gun he carried—he was here this morning, wasn't he? I saw the gun Eilert had with him, and I recognized it. It was yours! Well, Hedda, think of the scandal! The scandal of which you are so terrified. Naturally you'd have to appear in court—both you and Madame Diana. She'd have to explain how the thing happened. Did he threaten to shoot her, and did the gun go off then—or did she grab the gun, shoot him, and then put it back in his pocket? You'll have to answer the question. Why did you give Eilert the gun? And what conclusion will people draw from the fact that you did give it to him? [Ibsen, *Hedda Gabler*]

Lady Bracknell: Mr. Worthing, I confess I feel somewhat bewildered by what you have just told me. To be born, or at any rate bred, in a handbag, whether it had handles or not, seems to me to display a contempt for the ordinary decencies of family life that reminds one of the worst excesses of the French Revolution. And I presume you know what that unfortunate movement led to? As for the particular locality in which the handbag was found, a cloakroom at a railway station might serve to conceal a social indiscretion—has probably, indeed, been used for that purpose before—but it could hardly be regarded as an assured basis for a recognized position in good society. You can hardly imagine that I and Lord Bracknell would dream of allowing our only daughter—a girl brought up with the utmost care—to marry into a cloakroom and form an alliance with a parcel? Good morning, Mr. Worthing! [Wilde, *The Importance of Being Earnest*]

DON'T DASH! DON'T DAWDLE!
REGULATE YOUR RATE!

A typical concerto has three movements, which usually are to be performed fast, slow, and fast. But does this mean that when the composition is played, only three different tempos are used? Hardly. The general effect would be sheer ennui.

In the first section of his Piano Concerto No. 1 alone, Tchaikovsky indicates forty-four different variations of tempo. In the second and third movements, twenty-eight tempo patterns are suggested. Thus, in listening to a thirty-six-minute performance of the work, you'll hear about seventy-two different tempos, or approximately two contrasting rates of speed per minute.

Time or rate variations are as essential in reading and speaking as they are in music! Have you ever heard a speaker whose voice leaps upward, plunges downward, and never lingers on one pitch for more than two seconds? Yet in spite of all the acrobatics, he's still guilty of a certain tediousness.

Rate *includes the speed at which a person speaks, the length or duration of sounds, and the length and number of pauses.*

Measuring rate by counting the number of words read or spoken per minute (w.p.m.) is not entirely accurate, because words vary in length. But it can give you some idea.

In terms of w.p.m., Franklin Roosevelt clocked in at about 110 w.p.m. and John F. Kennedy at 180 w.p.m.

Martin Luther King opened his memorable "I have a dream..." speech at a pace of about 90 w.p.m., but finished at 150 w.p.m. Jimmy Carter, often described as a ponderous speaker—a drawler—averaged 160 w.p.m., and Ronald Reagan averages about 10 more w.p.m. than Carter.

Are You On a Fast Track Or a Slow Track?

16. Using a watch or clock with a second hand, time yourself carefully as you read aloud this folk tale.

THE THREE WISHES
A long time ago Jack, a poor woodsman, lived in a forest. Every day he chopped down trees. One day he came across the largest oak tree he had ever

seen. Said Jack, "There's enough lumber in this giant to build a whole house."

He raised his axe. Suddenly a tree sprite appeared. "I beseech you, spare this tree!"

Deeply moved, Jack replied, "Very well. Your tree is saved."

The sprite spoke. "To reward you I'll grant you your next three wishes—whatever they are."

When Jack got home, supper was not ready. He was hungry. "I wish I had a plump, juicy sausage."

A fat sausage dropped onto the table.

Said his wife, "Where did you get that sausage?"*

He told her the story about the sprite.

"What an imbecile you are!" she said. "Wasting a wish on a sausage! I wish it were stuck to your nose!"

And it was. He pulled and pulled, but the sausage wouldn't come off.* *

He had one more wish. He wished that the sausage would fall off his nose. It did. And if Jack and his wife didn't find themselves with loaded treasure chests, they at least had a delicious sausage for their supper.* * *

If it took you one minute to reach the single asterisk—120 words—you're snail-paced. Much too slow.

If it took you one minute to reach the triple asterisks—200 words—you're sprinting lickety-split. Much too fast.

If it took you one minute to reach the double asterisks—160 words—you're right on the nose. Moderate.

Don't Creep or Crawl! Don't Stall!

A speaking or reading rate of 120 to 140 w.p.m. can irk your listeners even more than the "faster-than-a-speeding-bullet" rate some hyperkinetic individuals use. It suggests that its user is ill, timorous, or stupid. (Actors playing not-too-swift characters often speak at a tortoise crawl.)

People can listen faster than you can talk, and if your rate is draggy or funereal, you'll soon lose their attention.

BE VIBRANT, VARIED, VIVID AND VERSATILE!

On the other hand, if your local Sesquipedalian Society invites you to give an after-dinner speech on "A Comparison of the Myoelastic-Aerodynamic and the Neurochronaxic Theories of Voice Production" you'd be wise to talk at 120 to 140 w.p.m. Complex, technical, sad, or profound matter works well at this rate.

17. Even though you'll rarely have an occasion to read or speak in slow motion, get the feel of it. The selection below contains exactly 140 words. The number of words up to the diagonal lines is 120. A maximum and a minimum are established. Practice, timing yourself, until it takes you close to a minute to reach either terminal point.

> All of you who live on after us, don't harden your hearts against us. If you pity wretches like us, maybe God will be merciful to you on Judgment Day. You see us here, five or six of us, strung up. As for the flesh we loved too well, it's already devoured and has rotted. And we, the bones, now turn to ashes and dust. Don't mock us or make us the butt of jokes. The rain has rinsed and washed us; the sun dried us and turned us black. Magpies and crows have pecked out our eyes and torn away our beards and eyebrows. Never are we at rest. The winds keep swinging us—now here, now there./ /
> Lord, keep us out of hell. There's nothing for us to do there! Friends, don't jeer! May God forgive us!
> [Villon, *Ballad of the Hanged*]

Don't Hasten or Hurry

A rate of 180 to 200 w.p.m. may exhaust your listeners. Burning up the road tells the world that you're highly nervous, unsure of yourself, or emotionally rattled. Faster speaking isn't necessarily better speaking. And have you noticed? We tend to be suspicious of fast talkers; we pigeonhole them as slick operators, shady lawyers, or high-pressure used car salesmen.

A fast rate, however, is proper for some humorous material, elation, excitement, fear, or anger. Even then—use it sparingly.

18. This selection contains 200 words; the diagonals are placed after the 180th word. Read it aloud to get a general idea of the tempos of 200 w.p.m. and 180 w.p.m.

> What is it, then? What do you want? What have you come for? What do you mean by this flightiness? Bursting in all of a sudden, like a cat having a fit! Well, what have you seen that's so surprising? What kind of an idea has gotten into your head? Really, you know, you act like a three-year-old child and not in the least like what one would expect from a girl of eighteen. I wonder when you'll get more sensible, and behave as a well-brought-up young lady should and learn a few good manners? Oh, your head's always empty! You're copying the neighbor's girls. Why are you always trying to be like them? You've no business using them as models. You have other examples, young lady, right in front of you—your own mother. I repeat—your own mother! That's the model you ought to imitate! There, now you see—it was all because of you, you silly child, that our guest was on his knees in front of me—proposing—then you blunder in./ /
> You come snooping around, just as though you'd gone completely out of your mind. Just for that, I refused him! [Gogol, *The Inspector General*]

Be A Middle-of-The Roader! Be moderate!

140 to 180 w.p.m. is the most tolerable and useful all-purpose rate. If you have to handle material that expresses sorrow, gravity, meditation, or material that is technical—aim for the lower end of the range: 140 w.p.m.

If your material expresses happiness, humor, or, on occasion, wrath, target the upper end of the range: 180 w.p.m.

BE VIBRANT, VARIED, VIVID AND VERSATILE!

Purely conversational situations? 150 to 180 w.p.m. is excellent.

Have to deliver a speech? Our best public speakers find that 160 w.p.m. is a congenial and efficient average.

19. The selection contains 180 words; the diagonals are placed after the 140th word. Practice at the different rates until you feel natural and at ease.

> In a churchyard in Nigg there is a plain, unmarked stone near which the caretaker never ventures. A wild tale connects the strange stone with a haunted ship which had no crew and which anchored in a nearby port. The plague, the story goes, was brought to the place by the ghost ship. One day the plague was seen flying along the ground in the shape of a little yellowish cloud. The whole country was alarmed, and groups of people watched with anxious horror the progress of the threatening, ominous cloud. They were saved by a clever citizen who owned an immense piece of canvas, shaped like a huge balloon. He cautiously approached the dreaded cloud and with great skill enclosed it in the bag. He wrapped it carefully, fold after fold, and then he secured it with many pins./ /
> As the canvas gradually started to change color, as if in the hands of a dyer, from white to yellow, the hero rushed it to the churchyard and dumped it into an open grave where it has slept ever since. [Folk Tale]

20. Look over the selections below and decide on a general rate that fits the mood of each piece of material. When you real aloud, however, make subtle changes in rate: accelerate, decelerate, hold steady:

> One dark and stormy night, a ship struck a reef and sank. But one of the sailors clung desperately

to a piece of the wreckage and was finally cast up exhausted on an unknown beach. In the morning he struggled to his feet and, rubbing his salt-encrusted eyes, looked around to learn where he was. The only thing he saw that could have been made by man was a gallows. "Thank God!" he shouted. "Civilization!"

If it had not been for these things, I might have lived out my life, talking at street corners to scorning men. I might have died, unmarked, unknown, a failure. Now we are not a failure. This is our career and our triumph. Never in our full life can we hope to do such work for tolerance, for justice, for man's understanding of man, as now we do by an accident. Our words, our lives, our pains—nothing! The taking of our lives—lives of a good shoemaker and a poor fish peddler—all! That last moment belongs to us, that agony is our triumph! [Bartolomeo Vanzetti, letter to his son]

Cyrano: My nose is very large? Young man, you might say many other things, changing your tone. For example—"Sir, if I had a nose like that, I'd cut it off!" Friendly: "You'd have to drink from a tall goblet or your nose would dip into it." Descriptive: " 'Tis a crag...a peak...a peninsula!" Graciously: "Are you so fond of birds that you offer them this roosting place to rest their little feet?" Quarrelsome: "When you smoke a pipe and the smoke comes out of your nose, doesn't some neighbor shout 'Your chimney is on fire'?" Warning: "Be careful, or its weight will drag down your head and stretch you prostrate on the ground." Tenderly: "Have a small umbrella made to hold over it, lest its color fade in the sun." My friend, that is what you'd have said if you had had some learning or some wit. But wit you never had a bit of. As for letters, you have only the four that spell out "fool!" [Rostand, *Cyrano de Bergerac*]

Dorine: If you ask me, both of you are insane. Stop this nonsense, now! You do want to marry each other, don't you? Mariane, surely you don't want to

BE VIBRANT, VARIED, VIVID AND VERSATILE!

marry the quack—that imposter—your father has picked out for you? So stop fussing and be quiet. You two are like all other lovers—you're crazy. Your father's a tyrant, and he has a plan we've got to stop. He's acting like a dunce. You'd better humor the old fossil. Pretend to give in to him. Tell him you'll marry the man he wants you to marry. Then keep postponing the wedding day. That way you'll gain time, and time will turn the trick. Your father is the most superstitious man I've ever known. He believes in omens and dreams. The day before your wedding, tell him that you had a dream the night before about a hearse and a funeral or that you broke a mirror or that a black cat crossed your path. He'll call off the wedding! But if everything else fails, no man can force you to marry him unless you take his ring and say "I do." That's the scheme. Now get going! There's no time to chat. Come on, now! Walk! [Molière, *Tartuffe*]

Squeeze and Stretch!

Words and syllables are squeezeboxes. Like accordions, they can be expanded or compressed. When do you squeeze and when do you stretch?

21. For demonstration purposes, read the following excerpts from two of the most popular poems in the English language:

"Now, Dasher! now, Dancer! now, Prancer and Vixen!
On, Comet! on, Cupid! on, Donder and Blitzen!
To the top of the porch, to the top of the wall!
Now dash away, dash away, dash away all!"
   ["A Visit From St. Nicholas," Clement C. Moore]

The curfew tolls the knell of parting day,
The lowing herd winds slowly o'er the lea,
The ploughman homeward plods his weary way,
And leaves the world to darkness and to me.
         ["Elegy Written in a Country Churchyard,"
                                    Thomas Gray]

As you read the Moore poem, you slashed and shortened most of the vowels and diphthongs. But with Gray's "Elegy," you instinctively lengthened and extended most of the vowels and diphthongs.

In a real-life, nonpoetic situation, how would you shout this one? "Hey! The house is on fire! Quick, somebody, call for help!"

You'd attack each word as though you were touching a hot stove. You wouldn't loiter long. For such brisk, riveting-machine attacks, let's borrow the word *staccato* from musical terminology. A *staccato* treatment of words is relevant if you're trying to express extreme emotional states such as rage, fright, enthusiasm, and joy.

Now pretend you're hypnotizing somebody and say: "Relax. Close your eyes. Go to sleep."

You gave it a *legato* treatment—the opposite of *staccato*. *Legato* describes a smooth, connected style, but it also implies that words are prolonged or "drawn out."

A *legato* treatment is what you want if you're dealing with calmness, reverence, awe, or deep grief.

Now say: "I'm going shopping. Want to come along?"

Staccato? No. *Legato?* Hardly.

Regular? Yes. Let's use the word regular for matter-of-fact, offhand, routine conversation and speech.

22. These lines are marked S for *staccato*, L for *legato* and R for *regular*. Read them accordingly. Notice the contrasts.

    S: I can't stand it another minute!
    L: The lake is sad and calm tonight.
    R: Oh, I wish I had that kind of money.
    S: Look out! He's got a gun! Duck!
    L: I don't know how to tell you this, but I've always loved you.
    R: May I see you later this evening?

BE VIBRANT, VARIED, VIVID AND VERSATILE!

S: Get out of here and don't ever come back.
L: Get out of here and don't ever come back.
R: Get out of here and don't ever come back.

23. You're on your own!
Study each of these sentences and then give it the interpretation you think most apropos. Want to be ingenious? "Shift gears" within a line, going from a *legato* to a *staccato* or *regular* reading.

I'm sorry, but he died quite peacefully two hours ago.
This is the last time you'll ever try anything like that.
I've never heard of anything like this before, have you?
Give me three minutes to think it over and you'll have your answer.
That movie was the longest, dreariest bore I've ever sat through!
Excited? Who's excited?
Don't ever let me catch you in that place again.
I thought I told you to leave town, partner!
It's a lazy, hot and humid day.
She was such a decent person ... quiet, patient. We couldn't have known that she was slowly dying.

THE PAUSE THAT REFRESHES

A **pause** is a rest stop—a period of silence.

Almost every performer from Lassie to Luke Skywalker knows exactly how Hamlet should be played. Maybe that's one of the reasons it isn't always well played. The popular Hamlets of John Gielgud, Richard Burton, Laurence Olivier, Richard Chamberlain, and Derek Jacobi have been greeted with standing ovations. Some Hamlets have been hissed and booed.

Hamlet's most universal moment is his famous meditation

on death, the "To be or not to be..." soliloquy. There are recordings available of Gielgud, Burton, and Olivier. If you have a chance to listen to any of them, you'll notice curious differences in the location and length of pauses.

A former student of mine, Robert Milli—now a stage and TV actor—played Horatio to the late Richard Burton's Hamlet. Burton delivered a different performance each night! On three consecutive evenings he gave completely dissimilar readings of the soliloquy:

To be   or not to be   that is the question.
To be or not to be   that is the question.
To be or not to be   that   is the question.

Which is the most eloquent? Probably none is better than others. Taste alone, not rules, can decide.

Nevertheless, something tells us that we would be annoyed with these readings:

To   be or not to   be that is the question.
To be or not   to be   that is the   question.

(With no pauses at all) Tobeornottobethatisthequestion.

The late Hubert Humphrey, 1968 presidential candidate, talked faster than a bat out of hell, with virtually no pauses. Former President Gerald Ford quipped: "Listening to Hubert is like trying to read *Playboy* with your wife turning the pages."

Why Pause?

For clarity.

Read these twice. The first time, ignore the pause marks. The second time, pause where indicated.

When Ann had eaten / / the dog ran away.
Hank, her date / / said Bob / / was quite boring.

Without the pauses, they're confusing. (Ann ate the dog? Who was boring—Hank or Bob?)

For emphasis and emotional quality.

Again, read these twice, without pauses and with pauses. There's a vast difference.

BE VIBRANT, VARIED, VIVID AND VERSATILE!

We shall fight on the beaches / / we shall fight on the landing grounds / / we shall fight in the fields and in the streets / / we shall fight in the hills / / we shall never surrender.

How do you know love is gone / / If you said that you would be there at seven, and you get there by nine, and he or she has not called the police yet / / it's gone. [Zsa Zsa Gabor]

To take a break and take a breath.

If you insist, you can read the next paragraph on one breath, but you won't be comfortable. Take the pause, and you won't expire!

I expect to pass through this world but once. Any good therefore that I can do, or any kindness that I can show to any human being / / let me do it now. Let me not defer or neglect it, for I shall not pass this way again.

24. Gulp but don't gasp!

Believe it or not, you can make sense out of the nonsense below—*if you pause in the right places.* You'll need to gulp some air while you're reading, but don't gasp for breath in the middle of a phrase.
Have fun!

Esau Wood sawed wood. Esau Wood would saw wood. All the wood Esau Wood saw Esau Wood would saw. In other words, all the wood Esau saw Esau sought to saw. Oh, the wood Wood would saw! And oh, the wood-saw with which Wood would saw wood. But one day Wood's wood-saw would saw no wood, and thus the wood Wood sawed was not the wood Wood would saw if Wood's wood-saw would saw wood. Now, Wood would saw if Wood's wood-saw would saw wood, so Esau sought a saw that would saw wood. One day Esau saw a saw saw wood as no other wood-saw Wood saw would saw wood. In fact, of all the wood-saws Wood ever saw saw wood Wood never saw a wood-saw that would saw wood as the wood-saw Wood saw saw wood would saw wood, and I never saw a wood-saw that would saw as the wood-saw Wood saw would saw until I saw Esau saw wood with the wood-saw Wood saw saw wood. Now Wood saws wood with the wood-saw Wood saw saw wood.

How'll You Have Your Pause—Medium, Rare, or Well-done?

The pregnant pause—also known as the dramatic pause—is an understated way of bringing out meanings or emotional content. Ronald Reagan, Billy Graham, Jesse Jackson, and Jane Fonda are clever in their use of this kind of pause.

Polished conversationalists and public speakers understand the importance of the pregnant pause. So do actors. George C. Scott once said that not only is the pause the most precious thing in speech but it is the last fundamental that the actor masters.

The provocative thing about the dramatic pause, however, is not its frequency but its length. Solemn, profound, and complex subjects generally need longer pauses than lighthearted, unpretentious, or familiar material.

25. A long pause *after* an idea or a phrase underscores what has just been said:

    If God had wanted us to think with our wombs, why did He give us a brain? I don't mind living in a man's world as long as I can be a woman in it. God made man, and then said I can do better than that and made woman. I'm not radical. I'm just aware. / / I've come a long way, baby! [Jane Fonda]

26. A long pause *before* an important idea or a climactic key word heightens suspense:

    Only one person could have killed her, and that person is / / you.

BE VIBRANT, VARIED, VIVID AND VERSATILE!

27. If you're trying to be funny or humorous, the punch or laugh line can often be pointed up and made funnier if it's preceded by a protracted pause. The late Laurel and Hardy were past masters of this kind of timing. Stan Laurel (the thin one) said on his deathbed, "Dying is hard, but not as hard as playing comedy."

Bill Cosby, Carol Burnett, and Eddie Murphy are also particularly adept at accentuating their punch lines.

As a simple example of how to point up a line, try:

Rock Magazine recently took a poll to name the best-dressed rock star. / / Nobody won.

Caution: Punctuation is generally a guide for the eye rather than the ear. True, you sometimes pause where a writer has placed a comma or a dash, but not always. If you pause for every punctuation mark, you'll sound jerky and choppy. Pauses, in themselves, are *silent* punctuation marks.

28. In this material, /L/ indicates a long pause, /M/ a medium pause, and /S/ a short pause. These are suggestions only. Obviously, long, medium, and short are comparative terms.

What is the most important thing in the world? /L/ Love.

If you watch a game, it's fun /S/ if you play it, it's recreation /M/ if you work at it /L/ it's golf.

Sunday School /S/ a place where they tell children about God for fifty-one weeks /L/ and then introduce them to Santa Claus.

One out of four people in this country is mentally unbalanced. /S/ Think of your three closest friends. /M/ If they seem okay /L/ then you're the one. [Ann Landers]

Eating is self-punishment. /L/ Punish the food instead. /M/ Strangle a loaf of bread /S/ throw darts at a cheesecake /S/ chain a lamb chop to your bed /S/ beat up a cookie. [Gilda Radner]

And there it lay /M/ that moldy coffin /S/ ugly and menacing in the bloodless moonlight. /S/ We lurched forward. Six pairs of trembling hands seized the grimy lid /S/ ripped it open. /M/ Something /S/ somewhere shrieked. /M/ Our eyes, hot and glazed, pierced the formless shadows inside the casket. /S/ Again a godless scream and then we knew /M/ the evil box /S/ was /L/ empty.

29. Analyze these selections for location and length of pauses. Mark according to your own judgment and then read.

Lillian Gish, when asked on her eightieth birthday about the secret of her longevity: "Keep breathing."

When I'm happy I feel like crying, but when I'm sad I don't feel like laughing. I think it's better to be happy; then you get two feelings for the price of one.

[Lily Tomlin]

Politicians are the same all over. They promise to build a bridge even where there is no river. A politician thinks of the next election; a statesman of the next generation. Anyone can be elected once by accident. Beginning with the second term, it's worth paying attention.

[Shirley Chisholm]

I find TV very educational. The minute somebody turns it on, I go into the library and read a good book.

[Woody Allen]

It is perfectly monstrous the way people go about nowadays saying things against one, behind one's back, that are absolutely and entirely true.

We travel all over the world to find beauty. But unless we carry it with us, we'll never find it. There is beauty in everybody. You are born with it. It's just

GETTING YOUR ACT TOGETHER

a matter of what you do with it, and if you lose it, it's like losing your soul.

"Take care of the sense," Lewis Carroll wrote, "and the sounds will take care of themselves."

You've covered much ground in this chapter: range and rate, pitches and pauses, staccato and legato, slides and glides.

Blend and weave them together as you work on the exercises below. Don't get hung up on devices! What is the general effect you're trying to achieve? Search for meaning and intelligibility. Search for various feelings and moods. Above all, search for freshness and spontaneity.

30. Use all the vocal versatility you can muster. Be original. Give each selection a little razzmatazz!

Micio: You're wrong! Believe me, it's not a terrible crime for a young man to indulge in wine and women. It isn't, really! Listen to me, and don't din this into my ears. You have given me your son to be mine by adoption. He has become my son! If he does wrong, that's my business. I'll pay the expenses. Supposing he makes love, drinks too much wine. I'll pay! Supposing he keeps a mistress, I'l pay! As long as I find it convenient, I'll let him have all the money he wants. If I don't find it convenient, I know exactly what will happen. She'll slam the door in his face. The long and short of it is—quit interfering! You slammed the door in his face, didn't you? Mind your own business, because if you don't, I can certainly prove that you are far more to blame for this mess than I am. [Terence, *The Brothers*]

Prudence: Oh, I've always known it would turn out like this! I felt it in my bones. I knew something marvelous was going to happen the day you came here. And what's more, I can always tell a married man from a bachelor. And I knew that you were dying to get married. How did I know? Last night I dreamt that I was at your funeral. When you dream about a funeral, it's always a sure sign of a wedding. And I knew from the first that you were a farmer, too. Oh, I know all about feeding chickens and laying eggs and milking cows and all that sort of thing. I adore, absolutely adore farmers!... What did you just say? You're not a bachelor? You're not a farmer? Well, I knew the day you came here you were nothing but a liar! [Ritchie, *Fashion*]

Orgon: You were a miserable pauper, and I saved you from starvation. I housed you. I treated you like a brother. I gave you almost everything I own. But just hold on, my friend, not so fast! A little more caution on your part! So you thought you'd fool me? You tried to act like a saint! You're not cut out to be a saint, and you got tired of your little act sooner than you thought you would, didn't you? Trying to marry my daughter, and worse, trying to seduce my wife—right under my nose. I've been suspicious for a long time, and I knew I would catch you in the act. And you've given me all the evidence I need. It's enough! And I don't need any more talk from you. Spare me your lies, and get out of here! [Molière, *Tartuffe*]

Martha: My husband—dead? That dear man! Not really dead? Oh, help me—I may faint! Wait! Do you have the evidence I need? I want a death certificate. I want to know where, when, and how that miserable creature died. What did he say on his deathbed? Didn't he send anything to me? A few gold coins, perhaps? A ring or two? He deserted my bed and board three years ago. But that dear, sweet man... I forgive him. Oh, I'll be a widow for a year—well, maybe not for a whole year—then I'll look around for another man. It won't be easy finding one like him. No woman on the face of this earth had a sweeter fool than mine. If only he hadn't roamed around so much. He was never home. And he couldn't resist that foreign wine. Not to mention those foreign women. And those damnable dice! He had a passion for rolling them. Why, that wretch! To rob his children and his wife! May his soul rot in hell! [Goethe, *Faust*]

Dion: Look at you! You, a man with one foot in the grave, sitting there and kissing that lovely girl! Don't you like to kiss your own wife? How do you intend to explain this to her? You'll lie to her, won't you? You'll tell her it's only fatherly kissing, I suppose. Ha! And all that money you have? You stole it from your wife, didn't you? I'll be damned if I'm going to keep my mouth shut about this. I'm going straight to your wife and tell her that you're going to strip her bare unless she stops you—and stops you right now! [Plautus, *The Comedy of Asses*]

Julia: Have I had any other happiness in this world except to smooth your way for you, nephew? You, who have had neither father nor mother to depend on. And now we have reached the goal, George! Things have looked black enough for us, sometimes. But, thank heaven, now you have nothing to fear. And the people who opposed you—who wanted to bar the way for you—now you have them at your feet. They have fallen, George. Your most dangerous rival—his fall was worst. And now he has to lie on the bed he made for himself—that poor, stupid, misguided creature. [Ibsen, *Hedda Gabler*]

Post Mortem

> I ain't as good as I should be;
> And I ain't as good as I'm going to be;
> But I'se better than I was!

You've done the *before*.

In Chapter 1 I suggested that for your initial recording you put a sample of your voice on a special segment of tape and save it. As you listened to that first taping, what were the **target areas** you set up for yourself, using Checklist B in Chapter 1?

TARGET AREAS:

Now it's time for the *after*.

Re-read one of the three selections in Chapter 1. Or repeat whatever material you used for that first recording. If possible, place your new segment right next to the older one.

As you prepare for your *after* performance, forget the hocus-pocus. Think about general improvement. Be natural and uncontrived. Give it an impromptu touch. *Put your best voice forward!*

For a fascinating comparison, play back your original performance first and then your current one. Along with your staunch and steadfast sidekick, use this checklist to monitor your overall improvement:

Make two photocopies (one for your listening friend) and use them to fill out the following.

FINAL CHECKLIST

QUALITY
___ **Substantial improvement**
___ **Moderate improvement**

LOUDNESS
___ **Substantial improvement**
___ **Moderate improvement**

ARTICULATION
___ **Substantial improvement**
___ **Moderate improvement**

EXPRESSIVENESS
___ **Substantial improvement**
___ **Moderate improvement**

UNOBTRUSIVENESS
___ **Substantial improvement**
___ **Moderate improvement**

If you've made substantial improvement in your target areas, congratulations!

If you've made moderate improvement in certain areas—if you feel there's room for still more improvement—stay with it!

Let a unique and ubiquitous seventeenth century Swedish queen give you a little gem of commonsensical advice:

"It is necessary to try to surpass one's self always; this occupation ought to last as long as life."

[Queen Christina]

Index

Accent, 17–19
Alabama speech, 18
Anderson, Judith, 21
Andrews, Julie, 12
Animation, 16–17, 153–154
Appalachia, 129, 134–135
Articulation, 3, 14–15, 39, 71–75
    consonants in, 67–71, 75, 81, 82, 93, 116–117, 119
    labored, 17
    in nasality, 55, 57
    poor, 66–67, 93

Baltimore speech, 18, 77, 128, 142
Battle, Kathleen, 12
Bell, Alexander Graham, 124
Bogart, Humphrey, 72
Bori, Lucretia, 64
Boston speech, 18, 91
Breath control, 26, 30, 53
Breath stream, 101, 107, 124
Breathiness, 13, 40, 41–46, 47
Breathing, 3, 25–32, 48, 49–50
    pauses and, 189
Brokaw, Tom, 18, 20

Bronson, Charles, 50
Brothers, Joyce, 17
Buckley, William, 67
Buddy System, 2
    See also Friendly critic, use of
Burnett, Carol, 46, 191
Burns, Robert, 10
Burton, Richard, 21, 187, 188

Cagney, James, 111, 179
Carroll, Lewis, 193
Carter, Jimmy, 21
Central (deep) breathing, 26, 27, 28, 48
Chamberlain, Richard, 187
Chancellor, John, 12
Checklist, 5, 6–7, 195, 196
    voice evaluation, 21–22, 24
    vowel, 126–27
Chin position, 51, 61
Chung, Connie, 12
Clarity, 188
Clavicular-shoulder breathing, 26–29, 48
Collins, Joan, 12
Communication, 7, 10, 67

INDEX

Compression of words, 185–187
Connery, Sean, 12
Consonants, 44–45, 66–123, 124
Conversation, 7, 164, 183
Cosby, Bill, 191
Cosell, Howard, 174
Country singers, 13, 54

Deep breathing. *See* Central (deep) breathing
De Gaulle, Charles, 114
Delaware speech, 18
Denasality, 59–61
Derek, Bo, 42
Dialects, 17–19, 91, 104, 111–112
    See also Regional speech patterns
Diana, princess of Wales, 47
Diction, 3, 14
    See also Articulation
Diphthongs, 124, 126–127, 139–146, 159
    in projection, 152–153
Disraeli, Benjamin, 13
Duration of sound, 179

Eastern speech, 18–19, 111–112, 128, 141–42
Elizabeth, queen of England, 46
Emotional quality, 188–189, 190, 193
Emphasis, 188–189
English language
    as second language, 83, 92, 94–95, 114, 117
    sounds in, 68–69
Enunciation. *See* Articulation
Evans, Maurice, 174–175
Exercises, 2, 3, 4, 11
    breathing, 25–32
    consonants, 73–123
    lips, 38–39
    listening, 20–21
    loudness, 157–159
    melody patterns, 176–178
    quality defects, 41–65
    range, 162–163
    rate, 185, 186–187
    throat and mouth, 37–38
    Triple Play, 84, 95, 98, 100, 106, 107
    versatility, 193–195
Exhalation, 28, 29, 30
Expansion of words, 185–187
Expressiveness, 16

Ferraro, Geraldine, 46, 154
Fonda, Jane, 190
Ford, Gerald, 188
Foreign language, 83, 92, 94–95, 104, 114, 133
French language, 114
Fricatives, 71, 106–119, 120
Friendly critic, use of, 1–2, 3, 5, 41, 69, 147–148, 196
Frost, Robert, 20–21

Gabor, Zsa Zsa, 42
Garbling, 15, 17

INDEX

General (Standard) American dialect, 18–19, 131
German language, 94–95, 114, 117
Gielgud, John, 12, 187, 188
Gimmicks, 172–173
Glass, Lillian, 7–8
Glides, 70–71, 85–96, 168–170, 193
Graham, Billy, 154, 190
Gum ridges, 87, 88, 99, 105, 121

Hardy, Oliver, 191
Harshness, 13, 40, 50–54
Hartman, David, 18
Harvey, Paul, 12
Hawn, Goldie, 42
Haydn, Franz Joseph, 160
Hoarseness, 3, 14, 41, 64–65, 156
Houseman, John, 50
Humphrey, Hubert, 188

Inflection, 168–170
Inhalation, 26
Intelligibility, 193

Jackson, Jesse, 190
Jackson, Michael, 17
Jacobi, Derek, 187
Jaw, 36, 55
   in articulation of consonants, 72, 73–74
   in articulation of diphthongs, 140, 142
   in articulation of vowels, 128, 129, 131, 134
Jones, James Earl, 12
Jordan, Barbara, 47

Keaton, Diane, 42
Kennedy, John F., 21, 179
Kentucky speech, 18
Key, 164–168, 172
King, Martin Luther, 21, 179
Kissinger, Henry, 162

Laird, Charlton, 75
Landers, Ann, 47
Larynx, 48
Laurel, Stan, 191
Legato (treatment of words), 186–187, 193
Lewis, Carl, 11
Lips, 36
   in articulation of consonants, 71, 72, 73, 78, 90, 93, 97, 105, 109, 116, 119–120
   in articulation of diphthongs, 141, 143
   in articulation of vowels, 130–131
   exercises for, 38–39
Listening, 19–21
   to yourself, 175
Loudness, 1, 15–16, 47
   adapted to situation, 160
   levels of, 147–160
Lungs, 25–26

INDEX

MacArthur, Douglas, 164–165
Maryland speech, 18
Massachusetts speech, 17
Medical treatment, when to seek, 41, 59, 64, 156
Melody patterns, 173–178
Middle Atlantic speech, 18
Midwestern speech, 18, 131, 135
Milli, Robert, 188
Miracle of Language, The (Laird), 75
Mitchell, Leona, 11
Mitchum, Robert, 50
Monotony, 16, 161, 162
Monroe, Marilyn, 13
Mouth, 25, 37–38, 55, 57
  in projection, 151
Mumbling, 14, 17, 67–71
Murphy, Eddie, 191

Nasal passages, 59
Nasality, 2, 13, 40, 54–61, 128
Nasals, 55–56, 71, 96–106, 135–136
Nashville Network, 13
Nelson, Willie, 13
New England speech, 18, 91
New Jersey speech, 17
New York City speech, 17, 18, 91, 104, 128, 141–142, 143
Newton-John, Olivia, 12
Nicholson, Jack, 50
Nixon, Richard, 21

Oak Ridge Boys, 13
O'Connor, Sandra Day, 47
Olivier, Laurence, 21, 187, 188
Onassis, Jacqueline, 9

Parton, Dolly, 54
Patton, George S., 13
Pauley, Jane, 18, 20
Pause, 179, 187–193
Peck, Gregory, 12
Pennsylvania speech, 18
Personality traits suggested by voice, 9–10
  breathiness, 42
  harshness, 50
  loudness, 149, 150
  rate of speech, 180, 181
  stridency, 47
  throatiness, 61
Philadelphia speech, 128, 142
Pitch, 16–17, 49–50, 154–156, 159, 175, 193
  change of, 168–172
  key and, 164–168
Plath, Sylvia, 20–21
Plosives, 70, 76–85
Practice, 2, 11, 73
  rate, 181, 183
  See also Exercises
Pregnant (dramatic) pause, 190–193
Projection, 15, 16, 36, 54, 150–155
Punctuation, 191

Quality (voice), 12–14, 128
  defects of, 13–14, 40–65

INDEX

Quality (voice) *cont.*
 development of desirable, 36–65
 improvement in, 2, 10–12, 20, 196–197

Range, 162–163, 193
Rate of speech, 3–4, 178–185, 193
 projection and, 152–153
Rather, Dan, 18
Reagan, Nancy, 46
Reagan, Ronald, 21, 179, 190
Regional speech patterns, 17–19, 89, 91, 104, 141–142, 143
Regular treatment of words, 186–187
Relaxation, 32, 33, 36, 50, 51
Rivers, Joan, 13
Roberts, Pernell, 12
Robinson, Edward G., 111
Roosevelt, Franklin, 179

Sarnoff, Dorothy, 9
Sawyer, Diane, 20
Scott, George C., 13, 190
Shrillness, 9
Simpson, O. J., 72
Singsong, 173–174, 175, 176
Skinner, B. F., 33
Slides, 168–170, 193
Smoking, 64
Soft palate (velum), 82, 83, 96–97, 99, 101, 105, 122–123
Southeastern speech, 140

Southern speech, 18–19, 89, 131, 135, 140, 142
Southwestern speech, 18, 135, 140
Spanish language, 117, 133
Speaking voices:
 best, 12–17
 importance of good, 7–9
Speech, overlapping, 68
Spelling, 104, 113
Staccato (treatment of words), 186–187, 193
Stallone, Sylvester, 59
Steps, 170–172, 173
Streisand, Barbra, 12
Stridency, 3, 13, 40, 46–50
Subdialects, 19
Subject matter
 and rate, 181, 182–183
Surgery, 59, 64, 156

Tape recording, 1, 2, 3, 10, 41, 68–71, 124–127, 148, 175
 before/after, 11, 22, 196–197
Target areas (improvement), 24, 195–196
Tchaikovsky, Petr, 179
Teeth, 55
 in articulation of consonants, 71, 109, 112, 114, 120
Tension, 3, 36, 51
 in articulation of vowels, 128, 129
 and breathing, 27, 32–35, 42
 in throat, 47, 48, 50

INDEX

Texas speech, 18
Thatcher, Margaret, 47
Theresa, Mother, 46
Throat, 25, 36, 40, 51, 159
  constricted, 32, 47, 48, 50
  exercises, 37–38
  in projection, 155
Throatiness, 14, 41, 61–63
Time variations (reading), 179
"To A Louse" (Burns), 10
Tone, 12, 36, 47–48, 152, 170
  exercises, 39–40
Tongue position, 36, 51, 54, 55, 62
  in articulation of consonants, 71, 72, 73, 74–75, 82, 83, 87, 88, 89, 90, 99, 101, 102, 105, 107, 110, 112, 113, 114, 115, 120–123
  in articulation of diphthongs, 140, 141, 142, 143
  in articulation of vowels, 127, 128, 129–130, 132, 133, 134

Variety, 17, 161–195
Versatility, 161–195
Vibrancy, 161–195
Vocal abuse, 64, 154, 156–157
Vocal cords, 25, 41, 42, 113, 156
  and consonants, 75
  nodes on, 64
Vocal faults/foibles, 53
  consonants, 76–77, 80–81, 82–84, 86–88, 89–92, 93–94, 97–99, 101–105, 108–119
  diphthongs, 140–144
  "Irksome Quirks," 53
  vowels, 127–136
Voice as personal logo, 36
Voice personality, 4, 20
  See also Personality traits suggested by voice
Voice problems, 1, 2–4
Voice production, 25
Voiced consonants, 75, 107, 117–118
Voiceless consonants, 75, 107, 117–118
Volume, 15
  See also Loudness
Vowels, 49, 124–138, 159
  in projection, 152–153

Waggoner, Porter, 13
Wallace, George, 19
Wallace, Mike, 20
Walters, Barbara, 72, 90
Welles, Orson, 21, 50
West, Mae, 29
West Virginia speech, 18, 143
Western speech, 18